of hallelujah [B]

"Spirit will not
descend without
~ West African

foolsgold

fools

gold

MAKING SOMETHING FROM NOTHING
AND FREEING YOUR CREATIVE
PROCESS

•

Susan G. Wooldridge

HARMONY BOOKS / NEW YORK

Copyright © 2007 by Susan G. Wooldridge

All rights reserved.

Published in the United States by Harmony Books, an imprint of the Crown
Publishing Group, a division of Random House, Inc., New York.

www.crownpublishing.com

Harmony Books is a registered trademark and the Harmony Books
colophon is a trademark of Random House, Inc.

The following poems have been previously published: "Everything Breaks,"
"First Words," "Hitchhiker," and "Poppa's Rowboat" (originally published
as "Grandma's Rowboat") in *Bathing with Ants* (Boxcar Press, Cohasset,
California, 2004) and "Lunch" in slightly different form in *ONTHEBUS*,
Issue 17/18 (2002).

All permissions credits can be found at the back of the book on
pages 225 to 226.

Library of Congress Cataloging-in-Publication Data
Wooldridge, Susan, 1946–
Foolsgold : making something from nothing and freeing your creative
process / Susan Goldsmith Wooldridge.—1st ed.
1. Creation (Literary, artistic, etc.) 2. Self-actualization (Psychology)
3. Healing I. Title.
BF408.W66 2007
153.3'5—dc22

ISBN 978-0-307-34148-8

Printed in the United States of America

10 9 8 7 6 5 4 3 2 1

First Edition

to my parents, Ethel and Julian,
and to Chico Creek

CONTENTS

.

ACKNOWLEDGMENTS ···*xi*

INTRODUCTION AT CREEK'S EDGE ···*xv*

1 CREEKSIDE ALCHEMY

1 *wisdom beach*···*2*

2 *seaweed heart*···*7*

3 *moving the dishes*···*12*

4 *big toe: within arm's reach*···*19*

5 *queen of shell beach*···*23*

6 *touching down in pensacola*···*26*

7 *daffodils and w-3*···*30*

8 *one-mile moon and blaubeuren*···*36*

9 *oasis*···*41*

10 *on asking*···*44*

11 *poppa's owl*···*50*

.

12 *poppa's rowboat*...53

13 *creekside alchemy: gathering beauty*...55

14 *telephone kaddish*...60

15 *wrinkle nose*...65

16 *sweet surrender*...71

2

GOD'S MINI-STORAGE

17 *fellini: on giving up*...76

18 *damselflies emerging*...81

19 *freeing the creek*...86

20 *always green inside*...90

21 *the language of red*...96

22 *digging up the artemesia*...100

23 *god's mini-storage*...105

24 *poppa's ashes*...111

25 *godseye*...117

26 *angels in encinal: a pretty how town*...120

27 *first words*...125

28 *dragonfly haiku*...127

29 *mirror kiss: vernous*...131

30 *clock's breath*...135

31 *diamond dust*...139

32 *foolsgold and ethel's landing*...146

3   W O R L D   A S   S T U D I O

33 *being a horse* ... *152*

34 *bopper's songs: rolling with the muse* ... *157*

35 *the undersong* ... *162*

36 *nichtalelloudi: would you be willing* ... *165*

37 *ʒomoli* ... *171*

38 *write crazy love poems* ... *175*

39 *underground soup* ... *181*

40 *strawberries* ... *185*

41 *artist of plants* ... *187*

42 *entering the blue* ... *192*

43 *risking dance* ... *198*

44 *ooti and vov* ... *204*

45 *sun dog: flying heart in lost hills* ... *210*

46 *high hopes: the mermaid's daughter* ... *214*

47 *world as studio* ... *221*

48 *the only gold* ... *223*

ACKNOWLEDGMENTS

·

This book is the result of the love and perseverance of a
wonderful group of people. I thank you all from my heart of hearts.
The book would not be here without you.

My grown children, Daniel and Elisabeth, continue to delight and inspire me—as well as keep me in line—in writing and
in life.

My mother, Ethel Goldsmith, forever offers funny and
bright material. Her love, along with that of my father, Julian, no
longer here, has been a foundation for me.

For many years I've met on Wednesdays with my beloved
friend and writing partner Elizabeth Singh. She's kept me going
with astute, insightful, and sometimes dramatic encouragement.

If any of these chapters have coherence and focus it's also
due to my sister/friend and world-class writing consultant Jane
Staw (author of *Unstuck*). With gentle patience, she continues to
teach me how to write an essay. Again and again.

Arielle Eckstut, my agent and dear friend, patiently guided me through several incarnations of this book. Her husband, David Sterry, has been an inspiring coach and support.

My deepest thanks to the Harmony team. Shaye Areheart, my editor, has provided trust, love, and full freedom. Anne Berry is both sparky and reliable. She and Min Lee, who keeps me legal!, have been a delight to work with. Janet McDonald, copy editor, is a genius with a light touch and infallible ear. Dyana Messina, Kira Stevens, and the marketing team are gracefully introducing *Foolsgold* to the larger world. The design and production teams have patience, vision, and resourcefulness. Thank you also to the sales team and everyone else at Harmony Books.

What follows is in no particular order!

My friend Kathleen McPartland visited various offices with bright ideas and snacks throughout all phases of this work.

Sharon Paquin is always there, with heart, to send a healing prayer and blessings.

Joanne Allred refined the book with her wise poet's eye.

Maria Navarro Easton, another sister, is a playful model of how to live creatively in the world.

Wayne Pease has loyally helped me define what I'm doing from the beginning.

Deborah Woodard cheerfully fielded countless e-mails.

Heather Altfeld, with a finely tuned ear, led me to add several chapters as well as to deepen and pare down many pages, along with Kim Weir, who helped me focus and structure the book and finally let go!

Linda Hummel has become an indispensable friend and support.

Mark Johnson, bluesman extraordinaire, nourishes my spirit with his wonderful songs.

My neighbor Mandy Pyle's door is always open. Thanks, sweetheart.

Trudie Leap, what would I do without you? You too, Tanha.

Valley Oaks Village provides home, a circle of friends, and true, playful family. I wish I could name you all.

Ruth Younger gave astute last-minute editing help, along with Kiara Koenig, who offered keen encouragement and advice.

Ken Sepeda, Amber Miller, and Dave Hurst supplied great ideas, and Michael Goloff offered his fine gift with a camera.

Carol Southern, editor of *poemcrazy*, always a wise presence, taught me to ask the vital question "Does it serve the book?"

The folks at various cafés, especially my home base, Café Flo, along with Cal Java, Teaz Me, G'rilla Bites, Higher Ground, Peets, The Naked Lounge, and Bidwell Perk offer lively and nourishing offices.

My friends at Chico Natural Foods have sustained me with outstanding oatmeal, soup, sandwiches, and friendship for years. Special thanks to Arlene, Kevin, Rachel Oriana, Vince, Liza, Dale, Scott, Esther, and Rose. Thanks as well to the fine crew at S&S Produce.

Stephen Connors has given wise counsel for many years, as have Leah, Lila, Drew, Manu, Sheelah, and Esther, who are always there whenever I have the sense to go inside.

My dear friends and colleagues at California Poets in the Schools have provided the creative base for much of my work. You mean the world to me.

Much love and gratitude to the one and only Nancy Wiegman and my other yoga teachers, Patti, Amaera, and Rex, who help keep me in shape.

Blessings to my sterling dance teachers, Jeanne Christopherson, Deanna Figueroa, Nicole Ruff, Alaine Zinzou, and Djibril Camara (and thank you Jessa, Tanya, Tiffany, and all the drummers!).

Much love and thanks to other friends, colleagues, and family who continue to help in more ways than I can say, including:

Danielle Alexich, Cheryl Anderson, Vicki Artzner, Martha Bergland, Leonard Boehm, Season Braswell, Margaret Brett, Wendy Brown, Roxane Burnett, Carol Click, Chico VW (Willy and Kenny), Ruth Cooper, Cheryl Cozad, Judy Davis, Laura Denny, Joann Eckstut, Ellen Galena, the Gardners—Flo, Kate, Lew, Liz, and Mary—Bob Garner, Trish Garone, Liz George, John Goldsmith, Mary Goldsmith, Rich Goldsmith, Sue Nelson Goldsmith, Lisa Holeman, Lynn Jacobs, Cheryl Klein, Jill Lacefield, Lilananda, Tanha Luvaas, Heather Lyon, Jack Mabie, Kristin Mahlis, Mary Ann McDonald, the Matrix Energetics team, Paul and Frances Newsome, David Pierot, Sharyn Pierot, Kate Pinsonneault, Richard Platt, Diane Prince, Rosemary Quinn, Renee Renaud, Chris Reynolds, Kirk Ridgeway, Marilyn Ringer, Christi Rowe, Thomasin Saxe, Trish Schiesser, Dana Smith, Beth Spencer, Ryan Tranquilla, Gary Vincent, Tori Vincent, Patricia Wellingham-Jones, Kent Wooldridge, Kam Yuen, Monica Zukrow, and many others.

INTRODUCTION

at creek's edge

·

Don't ask yourself what the world needs.
Ask yourself what makes you come alive, and
then go do it. Because what the world needs
is people who have come alive.

—Harold Thurman Whitman

Today I have an hour to walk
by Chico Creek, time out for time in. Yellow sycamore leaves spin
into the water near my feet and float past. Some swish to creek's
edge and settle in like I do. I love to visit the edges of things where
worlds meet and merge. Much of *Foolsgold* has been written here
or at an "office" nearby that I share with the kingfisher and round
stones.

When I started the book, I was grieving the death of my father, the end of my long marriage, and the breakup of a subse-
quent romance. These pages show the ongoing practices and
experiences that bring me solace and delight and help me embrace

and begin to transform who I am in the world. *Foolsgold* tells the story of my personal creative process and encourages you to develop yours.

My love of foraging began when I was four. My father, a geochemist, took the family on field trips from Chicago to the wild west of Colorado and Wyoming. Dusty canvas pouches holding feldspar crystals tapped loose by narrow hammers weighed down the car's trunk. Enclosed and clattering, the faceted crystals seemed secret and precious to me. Poppa treasured every rock he encountered, even cubes of fool's gold, iron pyrite. Our field trips set my heart both on rocks and on time out in nature, gathering.

I began writing these pages when I decided to make a small collage box each day for a year with what I found on my walks— often the most ordinary, seemingly worthless bits of nothing. That's when fool's gold became foolsgold for me, a field around us, or state of being, where everything can be transformed by our seeing and creativity. Merged into one word, *foolsgold* describes a paradox, the value in what may seem to be worthless. Foolsgold reminds us to look beyond appearances, even in ourselves. What seems to loom in us most darkly may finally be what brings the most light. Everything can be transmuted by attention, play, love.

Celtic poet John O'Donohue suggests we make "an invitation to our soul to become visible." Sometimes our soul will shine through our creative work and we can have a peek. There's evidence of hidden treasure within us and all around—in the creek, the oaks, the bees, the day moon sliced in half as I walk along and let the day zing me with its light.

My creative process is sloppy and on the move. I do things in snippets and my "work" grows in increments. I may begin a poem about tree frogs or tape blue litter into my journal. I may plan a journey, meditate, or just sit and stare. One afternoon I plunked my abandoned gold wedding band in a collage box painted blue, where somehow it transformed into a simple gold circle with no beginning or end. I'd never known what to do with the ring. Where else could it go? Gold becoming foolsgold. Why not?

You'll find your own creative process. You might need order, quiet, and stretches of time at five in the morning. You might want a large canvas, a piano, or a collaborator. You might decide to shoot photos from the window of a train. And though your nature is boundless, you probably don't have boundless time. Maybe you have only five minutes! That's all the time it takes to make something from nothing, although you may extend the time to an hour, a day, or the rest of your life. With luck, these pages will encourage you to discover the process that suits you best, with the world as your studio.

We can't fool our hearts, and our creative hearts-way is alert, alive, tugging—sometimes even in our sleep. We do best to jot, sing, tape, glue, or paint whatever comes to us. The transforming state of being—the living flow—is what we're seeking, whether we know it or not. And somewhere during the process—maybe coming through grief or loss, as we release and notice and gather and create—we see it's not the end product we want, mere gold, it's the enlivening discoveries and delight we experience along the way. Foolsgold.

"There are beautiful and wild forces within us," St. Francis said. We can tap into them and encourage what physicist David Bohm calls the flow from the unseen to the seen that makes up the dynamic stream of creation, in what scientists are discovering to be a "participatory" universe.

I'm still here at the creek's flowing edge. Join me. Find your own creek's edge, whether it's in a garden, on a city street alive with talk, or in your zooming car—wherever you can sink into your being and allow creative life to flow through you.

I only went out for a walk and finally concluded
to stay out till sundown for going out, I found,
was really going in.
—JOHN MUIR

Solvitur ambulando. It is solved by walking.

—Saint Augustine

foolsgold

1

CREEKSIDE ALCHEMY

·

I went out to the hazel wood,
Because a fire was in my head,
And cut and peeled a hazel wand,
And hooked a berry to a thread . . .
—WILLIAM BUTLER YEATS

1

wisdom beach

.

A "no" uttered from the deepest conviction is
better and greater than a "yes" merely uttered to
please, or what is worse, to avoid trouble.

—GANDHI

I believe in the word *yes*. I resist
calling anything off—relationships, trips, any engagement. Today
I'm supposed to be in Arizona. Up to now I've often moved ahead
with such plans even when I've been heading toward rapids and
waterfalls with my heart shouting, "Stop!" Or at least, "Make a
U-turn!" If I hadn't canceled today's trip to a small family gathering at my brother's in Phoenix—where it's ten degrees hotter than
Chico's 105—I wouldn't be arranging my first collage day box
here by the creek, where I'm dabbling with a tube of blue paint and
a jar of Gorilla Glue mail-ordered from Restoration Hardware.
Circling water striders bounce light like sparklers near my feet,
and I feel my heart relax. Ahhh.

There's a terrific German word for my difficulty with yes and no: *Torschlusspanik,* literally "door shut panic"—fear of closing doors and letting go of options.

I'm learning to embrace the word *no,* for balance, for equilibrium, and to honor my intuition. Like a box, *no* provides walls and boundaries. It's a container, a framework in which creativity can come forth with controlled abandon. *No* stops me in its tracks and opens up a new place for me to begin. It can hold possibilities. Time for me and my ambling.

I've wandered to a sandy spot by the creek under an alder tree. I glue red roof-shaped plastic and a feathery pinwheel seed near the bottom of the Wells Fargo check box I tucked into my day pack and just painted turquoise. I add crumbling ash like islands in an aquamarine sea. A folded crimson bottle cap looks like the setting sun.

As I gather and glue, anxious gloom about missing things and not meeting expectations is slowly replaced with the calm thrill of being here by my wild creek making this—what is it? A collage journal mini-box? Damselflies, dragonflies, and butterflies swoop nearby. I've stepped through the looking glass.

I feel a flood of joy, an energetic rush, sensing that for now, this is my life's heart work, playing with words and colors and stuff and glue. There's something I need to discover here and I don't know where it will take me. Bringing my journal alive in small boxes feels like uncharted territory, a new world of possibility for me. I decide to make one a day for a year.

Someone left today's newspaper on a table by the creek, and I clip out the date with the scissors from my mini–Swiss Army knife and glue it down, *August 4.* A strip of paper catches my eye near my feet. I unearth a fortune cookie's small white promise, crumpled in the dirt, that proclaims, "You have at your command the wisdom of the ages." It's as if the Chinese sages planted a surprise message here for me. What sweet force and encouragement these words give my sloppy collage box! I plaster the fortune inside with Gorilla Glue. Why not? *The wisdom of the ages.*

The words remind me that the world will support me when I begin to practice my heart's desire. Soon I realize I *am* saying *yes,* an inner *yes,* supported and held in place by the outside *no.* Yes to doing what I want. Yes to how I feel. Yes to allowing time and space for grief about Poppa, the drawn-out ending of my marriage, and now a breakup with my crazy-love teacher, Jack—who reappeared in my life one month after my marriage ended.

This morning I'm finally listening to my heart, which for months has been suggesting that I make collages outside my journal—within small boxes, some painted blue. For now, objects speak the language of the heart as fully as images made of words. Colors, shape, stuff. Orange and black flicker feather, a silent poem in itself.

If I'd ignored my intuition and gone to Phoenix, I never would have had my day-box epiphany, or discovered the *yes* hiding inside my stubborn *no.* I wouldn't have found the fortune here at a place I'm naming Wisdom Beach. I wouldn't have this wild blue box that seems to be made by a creature and invites me to enter and dwell in a whole new realm where small things around me come to life as I arrange them in collage.

And I wouldn't be writing this book.

·

> After the final no there comes a yes.
>
> And on that yes the future world depends.
>
> —WALLACE STEVENS

WE ALL SAY *no* to ourselves too often, blocking creative expression from our lives. Learn to express how you feel and what you need so others understand. Find time for yourself every day even if it's late at night or early in the morning. Set aside just fifteen minutes; that's all you need to begin. Your creativity is there, waiting for you. Then, listen carefully for the *yes* that rises from deep within. This *yes* can open you up to art.

Write a list of everything you wouldn't do if you didn't think you had to. Write another list of what you'd do if you thought you had time. How can you make more time for your creative self? List ways to get help with the "must do" list. Your life may well depend on it. Where can you say *no* (or at least *wait*) to the outside world and *yes* to yourself? You can be polite.

The next time you're out walking, notice what catches your eye. You might carry a little sack for gathering, just for fun. If you want, choose a box to carry with you. It can be a checkbook box, a matchbox, or a white jewelry box you can drop in a pocket or a day pack. Often I'm happy with just the lid, like the round top of a Quaker oatmeal box or the top of a carry-out soup container. If you want more space, try a shoebox or the shallow top. You might like a flat piece of cardboard, paper, or wood. Play around with scale. I've been tempted to use the velvety inside of a discarded guitar case for fun. Choose any size that appeals to you.

Let the moon speak in your box. The sun. Pop-tops. Spiders.

.

Seeds. The heart. Let your box become a small world, and inside it (inside yourself), allow time for retreat. If that's what you want.

Well, friend, I hate to be the one to have to tell you this,
but you may be an artist.

—DAN WOOLDRIDGE

2

seaweed heart

.

To learn about the invisible, look at the visible.
— TALMUD

One New Year's Eve I resolved to follow my heart. The next day, as I walked along the creek, I was charmed by a piece of sky-blue gum trampled in the shape of a perky, cartoon-like heart on the cement at Chico's One-Mile Park. A heart in blue pajamas, I thought. My own heart felt wide open. Poppa was dying, my marriage was over, I was in love. When I resolved to follow my heart, I meant the loving part of me in touch with my deepest self. I didn't mean a blue gum heart. And though I know the world speaks to me through what I see, I didn't expect quirky, visible hearts to show up all over the place, leading me on a treasure hunt from leaf to petal to hawkmoth to the heart-shaped nose of a neighbor's purring cat.

For more than a year before I began to make collage boxes, I carried a camera everywhere, framing heart shapes I spotted in cracks in dirt, melting snow, drops of paint on the street, puddles, bark, beets, walnuts, deer prints in mud, and even in the collapsed plaster of a friend's ceiling. I took photographs from airplanes of clouds and landforms: ravines, meadows, hillsides, and valleys. I put together a book of words and photos called *A Field Guide to Wild Hearts* that never made it out into the world.

But seeing hearts is one thing; acting from the open heart—where creativity settles and deepens until it finally comes forth as expression—is something else. The outside hearts popping up all around serve to remind me.

On the Southern California coast one afternoon a perfect leathery heart made of seaweed waited for me on the sand. I picked it up and watched a man paddle his yellow plastic kayak to shore through a seaweed drift. He ignored a fat Australian shepherd wagging his whole body in greeting and rushed up weathered stairs to the top of the bluff in rubber boot slippers, cradling a rolled, plump towel. "Whatcha got?" the fisherman's friends yelled. He unveiled a gasping dragon-head of a fish with huge, blank eyes. "*Cabezon!*" they exclaimed. The fish was still alive. The fisherman lifted his catch for a camera and fins flopped open like palm fronds or cat claws on the upside-down lionfish.

His heart's still beating, I thought, and remembered watching Poppa "clean" fish in a shed on Little Lake Sissabagama in Wisconsin, walls and floor flecked with dry scales. He slit open the white belly to find the heart, the size of his pink fingertip, always still beating, slow and spasmodic, like a small creature. I've read that eggs begin to pulse with heartbeat before the chick heart is formed, animated by mysterious life force.

I guess if our hearts were always open, exposed like the seaweed, or like the sunfish heart beating in Poppa's palm, we'd be immobilized by vulnerability. But at least I can be aware of my pulse, sense the heart inside my body that often seems to have a mind of its own, reminding me, Sue, oh mind-heavy one, listen to me! Now, for heaven's sake!

Most of my life I've ignored my heart's impulses as if they were bothersome, as if my physical heart didn't exist. When I began watching for heart shapes, I noticed how my heart feels, reacts, and lives in my body. I began feeling my emotions more fully, including sadness and mourning. Maybe all this helped prepare me for Poppa's death. And maybe Poppa's dying is opening me to a more daring way of being.

Sitting in the dusk by the ocean at Shell Beach with the delicate seaweed heart like a dried lizard in my lap, I wondered if we can see beauty only through our hearts. I wondered if true freedom is forged by the creativity hidden in our hearts, always waiting for attention, waiting for a voice.

> . . . How he submitted—. Loved.
> Loved his interior world,
> his interior wilderness,
> that primal forest inside him,
> where among decayed tree trunks
> his heart stood, light green. . . .
> —RAINER MARIA RILKE

Is THERE ANYTHING causing you distress? Focus on how your physical heart feels inside and see what happens. Notice if you feel sadness or joy when you begin to tune in. If you feel tears coming, find a place and way to let them flow.

We need courage to do our creative work in the world, whatever that may be. Courage—holding *coeur,* French for "heart." Maybe we need whatever it takes to shock our hearts open and free us from fear. Maybe contact with primal creative forces bringing and taking life allows us to glimpse our bottomless creative natures.

Speak to your heart now and then. Scientists say there are brain cells in the heart. The beating of the heart, according to Stephen Harrod Buhner in *The Secret Teachings of Plants,* produces an electromagnetic field much more powerful than that created by the brain. He suggests that human consciousness may well be centered in the heart.

Write a letter to your heart. "Dear heart." It's good to do this in the middle of the night. Let your heart write back through you. You might not get answers. Just beginning to pay attention to your heart in your body is enough to help you begin to open to your heart's creative, healing ways.

Later you might want to write alternate lines.

My heart says/ my mind says/ my heart says/ my mind says.

You might want to add more detail.

My heart, dressed in (corduroy, marigolds, blue glass)/

surrounded by (bees, licorice, smoke),/

asks, wonders, shouts . . .

    It is only with the heart that we see rightly;

    what is essential is invisible to the eyes.

        ——Antoine de Saint-Exupéry

EVERYTHING BREAKS

Waves show us
ice shows us
finger nails toe
nails bridges quake
and break necklaces
snap and pearls roll
to corners
where ants
carry crumbs to tumbling
hills, tunnels, clouds
break hearts
and roofs collapse, tornadoes,
floods, sudden winds
at night sweep under
our doors breaking
all we've ever

f o o l s g o l d

.

held

together

—S.W.

Breakage, whatever its cause, is the dark complement

to the act of making, the one implies the other.

The thing that is broken has particular authority

over the act of change.

—Louise Glück

3

moving the dishes

·

When I let go of what I am,
I become what I might be.
—Lao Tzu

I didn't want the clutter of food, chairs, even a bed when my thirty-year marriage ended. I craved open space and slept on a borrowed futon on the floor, eye to eye with dust bunnies and an extra pillow propped against the electrical outlet so I wouldn't get over-amped. I meandered alone by the creek as often as possible and noticed that the squirrels didn't have furniture, either.

Our surroundings help express our feelings. I wanted the house empty to match my heart, bare, with no room for anything but white, cool light coming in. I craved barrenness. Not only was my marriage over, but my youngest child was leaving for college in a month. I was no longer a wife and was practically no longer a mother. One day I just lay down on my new balcony and decided to stay there forever, until I disappeared. This was a time of drought, grief, silence, and pause. Here was an empty house and an empty self.

Nevertheless my friend Jane, visiting from Berkeley, ferried me to Ginno's Appliances and made me buy an Amana refrigerator then and there. Next she escorted me to Nantucket, an elegant home-furnishing store, and insisted I buy two green wicker chairs on sale.

This furniture seemed too much, but one hot July night my son, Daniel, home for the summer, moved the dishes with me. I stared into the cupboards. Which cups to take, hanging on their hooks beside the sink? Leave the yellow plates? Yes. How many forks? We didn't pack glassware the way you're supposed to, swaddled in sheets of paper. We wriggled columns of plates and cups into boxes crammed in sideways next to cookbooks on top of Nanny's rose and gray afghan. Some we cradled loose on the front seat of my Honda.

The antique Russian teacup and saucer clack-wobbled between casseroles. Barely used Wedgwood wedding china veered in thick stacks. Our everyday dishes—the blue and white stoneware we actually used—were left squatting in the cupboards of the old house where they belonged, with my husband, who was staying. How could I move them?

The dishes and I rolled slowly around the edge of Chico's Lower Park to Valley Oaks Village on the other side of the creek in a mini-caravan. Dan followed tentatively in the Toyota van, a white blimp, with the park sound of crickets and tree frogs rising around, over, and through us, making the dusk huge and alive and our mission small, clattering with plates. I remember early evening sun eerily orange like a slice of melon or a flat bowl through the haze of foothill fires. Then I saw the moon, also orange, waxing like a broken plate; no—like a melon rind, a curved canoe; no—like a tusk, a night tusk waiting above the trees in a peachy glow.

I wondered, as we drove, if the soul of a house hides in the dishes. Dishes hold all that food, decades of meals, spoon to mouth, salads and fruits and stews and cakes and pies and eggs and toast on plates in a circle for years on an old round table. Anyhow, here was the move, no going back, transporting dishes whole and clacking from our family home to waiting hollow rooms with an echo, my new empty house with no food.

In my journal I wrote later:

> Tall blue glasses wait in the new kitchen. All the mess is left behind: spills in the garage, frayed towels tumbling from the laundry room, browning teapot with enamel chipping off. All resist the perfect new house. The rocker, faded pink, won't come. Nothing real wants to move. The husband, father, holds fast in the house with all the history and heart. The walls of the new house are laced with tiny flies like winged dust. My old friends the spiders haven't found a way to enter.

MOVING THE DISHES, clean and empty, helped me sense that nourishment would come. Tea, wine, soups, a new way of being. The dishes, hidden in cupboards, were an invitation. For a time, I needed emptiness to make room for a new start. How can the mysterious, redemptive creative force enter (and where does it come from, anyhow?) when our houses or selves are crammed, busy, overfull? We need to let go of everything that gets in the way of what needs to enter.

The creative, it seems, is spawned from emptiness. Giving over to silence, waiting, allowing, listening. Coming to emptiness may mean coming through grief. Something has been lost, a marriage, a child, a house, a city, a world. An idea of who we are. Whatever seems familiar, tried and true.

In the emptiness we might get an inkling—as if something lights up and twinkles—of how we'll begin to form and open to who we're becoming, who we most truly are. We need to leave space both for what we'll discover and what will emerge to discover us.

Sometimes I miss the original emptiness of my house ringing with promise. I love the peace I feel when my mind is empty. I love the blank first page in a journal sleek with possibility. I love carrying a small, empty box on a walk. My new file cabinet is still empty; I resist cramming it with old words in manila folders.

When my friend Tori's husband died, she took her house apart, dragging everything out, "ripping and tearing, pulling up carpeting, putting sand on the walls," she told me, gesturing with passion. "I wanted my inside and outside to finally match," she said. Tori often worked in the middle of the night. Before she could create (and now her house is a work of art), Tori had to empty the house (and herself) completely.

Notice what's overfull in your world right now. Bookshelves? Your head? Empty a day in your calendar, a drawer in your bedroom, a shelf in your refrigerator, to make room for something new.

Buy a new journal. Carry it around without words. Gather empty boxes and surfaces. For as long as you want, leave everything empty. Soon you'll see the whole world makes offerings.

This being human is a guest house.
Every morning a new arrival.
A joy, a depression, a meanness,
some momentary awareness comes as an
  unexpected visitor.
Welcome and entertain them all!
Even if they're a crowd of sorrows, who sweep
your house empty of its furniture,
still, treat each guest honorably.
He may be clearing you out for some new delight.

—RUMI

4

----

big toe: within arm's reach
·

Without stirring abroad one can know the whole
world; Without looking out the window
one can see the way of heaven.
The farther one goes the less one knows.
—LAO TZU

My big toe spontaneously began
to talk to my two-year-old son, Daniel, when my daughter, Elisabeth, was born. Dan was shocked that I was nursing his new sister,
who appeared in my lap out of nowhere. I felt like I needed to be
two people at once, sporting at least four arms. With no relatives
around to help and my husand, Kent, engrossed in his job, there
seemed to be no way I could lovingly mother my two small children at once.

Help was closer than I could have dreamed. As I remember,
Dan was "gentwy" driving his toy motorcycle over Elisabeth's

face while she nursed when my big toe cleared its throat and began to speak. My Big Toe transformed everything when it introduced itself in a high, piping voice and admired Dan's ever-present green motorcycle (or "mo-da da"). I didn't seem to have much to do with it.

Daniel and Big Toe became best friends and allies, thank God. All at once Dan had part of me dedicated to him alone. After all, his new sister couldn't say a word. And besides, Big Toe wasn't interested in "Wibebef," as Daniel called her. Big Toe loved—indeed, revered—Daniel, often saying "I don't know, what do *you* think, Dan?"

It must have been my heart that made Big Toe talk, just as our hearts inform our practices and our art. My two children were my art form for a time, my (obsessive) creative practice. I needed to nurture Elisabeth. Big Toe kept her brother safe and happy at the foot of the bed or wherever we happened to be. Even through a shoe Dan could inform and advise (as well as confide in) him. Him or her, that is. We never clarified Big Toe's gender.

My heart, with its own imagination, sympathetic to our plight, scanned the scene and found something not only nearby, but an ever-present part of my body, to save the day.

I like to work with what's right at hand. My friend Martha calls this "lazy-smart." On walks I gather what catches my eye along the way for collage. When I took art classes in my twenties, I perched in bed each night turning my arm, sketching my left hand at every angle. I began learning to draw by copying the mysterious hand-as-model in front of my face, with fingers reaching out or curled like spider legs or crabs.

·

After we moved to Chico, California, sometimes I drew with a stick dipped in India ink at the edge of the creek. Bare feet at creek's edge or in the garden often ended up in my drawing.

Today by the creek with Big Toe in the sand, a bit stubby, brownish pink (silent for years), I find what I need again in what's as close as my toe: a bit of weathered green glass, pale roots, a drift-twig I slant beside a toe-size pecan shell, and a delicate feather with a heart at the tip enlivening the small collage box I'm making.

A bee lands to drink on the wet sand near my feet. I work at random with small, worn things. I don't have to go anywhere or buy anything. I settle down in my own wild world and find everything I need here, as close as my toe.

WHAT CATCHES YOUR EYE NEARBY? So much is already *given*. I just broke off a branch poking me in the head where I sit by the creek and taped the leaves into my journal—from the smallest heart shape to the largest.

Head out on a walk. You might just step into your yard or onto a curb on the street where you live. You might want to carry a matchbox (and Elmer's glue). Notice what's at your feet. A colorful leaf? A tattered one? Scan for litter, a bit of blue or red or silver foil. Look for spots of color as you walk along the sidewalk. If it's raining or snowing, a leaf might fall or a feather drift down. In summer you might see different shades of clover, orange petals at the edge of the walk, or a dandelion going to seed.

Next time you're barefoot, gaze at your feet. Wiggle your toes. Especially if you have young children, one of your toes might have something to say.

The moment one gives close attention to any thing, even
a blade of grass, it becomes a
mysterious . . . indescribably magnificent
world in itself.

—HENRY MILLER

5

queen of shell beach

·

Tired of speaking sweetly,
Love wants to reach out and manhandle us,
Break all our teacup talk of God.

—HAFIZ

Eroded cement stairs lead me to
a cove I love on Shell Beach where I like to jog when I drive to
Southern California. This morning I ask the ocean what she has
to tell me as I run along the edge of waves, journal in hand, keys
rattling in a pocket with my pen.

Everything shifts, waxes and wanes, loops around, the ocean
says, eager to speak to me. Pay attention to high tide and low, ebb
and flow, sudden storms as well as sunny breezes. Be alert to rip-
tides and squalls as well as rapture and floating.

Suddenly aware of people watching from the bluff above, I
become self-conscious and stop paying attention to the ocean. I
miss warning hints as the waves get larger and the tide comes up.

Darting in and out at the edge of the water, I forget the ocean's erratic rushing and suddenly, in too deep, I'm smacked by a wave and slapped against rocks as the sea snatches up my pen and my keys are swept away on their leather bootlace.

I scramble out of the undertow to higher ground with scraped, salty ankles stinging. Shaking sand out of my journal, I gently separate stuck-together pages where ink bleeds blue-black on salty, rippled paper.

The people up on the bluff help out. Rob finds a broken fishing pole and pokes around in water-rushed rocks, searching in vain for the keys with me, soaked to the knees. Sandy calls AAA on her cell phone and Ken shows up in a tow truck and breaks into my car, where I've left my bag and, thank heavens, extra keys.

Finally, before I leave, I turn my attention back to the ocean like a little kid approaching the forbidding realm of a powerful, unpredictable enchantress.

I have your keys below blue-gray waters, she tells me now. For a moment there, hot stuff, you thought you were in charge. For God's sake, if you pay attention I give warning signs and signals.

The ocean holds the answers, she wants me to remember. When we're together, she wants my full attention. That's the word she stresses, *attention*. Be handmaiden, I'm admonished. I notice that she took my pen. Like the deep unconscious, she's a source of art, writing, music, every form of life and inspiration. The large heart, the bottomless ocean inside and out. Don't take too much credit for your cleverness or writing, she says. Just pay attention.

If I pay attention, she'll fill me with inspiration. *She's* the wild queen, charging blue green, filled with hidden pearls, jelly-fish, men-o'-war, whales, poems, symphonies, paintings, phosphorescent plankton, sunken treasure, seahorses, sudden storms, and stolen keys wearing smooth in the tide of a full moon on Shell Beach.

> Sea and ocean are small, helpless words in the face of
> the wild divinity of the ocean. It always surprises you
> when you least expect.
> —JOHN O'DONOHUE

OUR BODIES—especially our knees—hold some of the same receptor cells that alert animals to earthquakes and other shifts in nature. Elephants broke their chains and ran for higher ground well before a great tsunami devastated much of coastal Sri Lanka, India, and Thailand. When we tune in and pay attention both to our own heart as well as to signs in nature and the behavior of animals around us, we tap a knowing that can keep us in tune, safe, and connected to our deep creative wells.

Whenever you can, feel your consciousness sink down into the area of your heart. Pay attention to the world from there. How's the weather informing you? The mountains, the creek, lake, sea? Your knees? How are the birds acting? We can be informed by beehives, eggs, all the visible and invisible worlds. We can gather this into our journals and our hearts.

6

touching down in pensacola
·

The eye becomes the ear and the ear becomes the
eye. They vibrate transparent. You work not
with the five senses but with the twenty senses
of the poet, the forty senses.
—GONZALO ROJAS

Here on a dock near Pensacola,
Florida, I've set about catching a great blue heron in my journal,
painting him with words. Lean, lanky, and alert, he's hand-fed by
local fishermen and allows me to come close if I'm slow and quiet.
I call him Hank, though he's glorious and regal like a King Henry.
Chest feathers open on his breast like a palm frond or a long fan,
and we size each other up, speechless. His yellow life-saver eyes
don't blink. When he swallows, a ripple moves down his S-curve
snake throat with a herringbone pattern—black, white, and gray.
Hank is knock-kneed elegant, with long toes splayed on thin leg

branches. His beak, aimed at me, is an arrowhead, a wedge, the prow of a long, low kayak.

Hank's head moves from side to side now and then, and long quill feathers flutter on his breast over drumstick thighs. One foot lifts delicately as I sense he's getting bored with me, lowly fisherwoman of language, offering no fish, only fish words: *gill flipper fin bone heart splash dart.*

What the heck, I decide to ask Hank, am I doing on a dock in Pensacola?

Touching down, Hank seems to say after a pause.

What can I learn from a blue heron? Be still. Be wary. Watch. Listen. Fly low to decide where to touch down. Trail your feet. Swoop. Open your mouth, a scoop.

Below, thousands of leery fish dart, pause, dart, pause, catching light on teardrop backs. Follow them. Never touch down far from water. And then, tune in.

Smell the sea. Feel the splintery dock underfoot. Notice your senses are engaged, all five, six, seven, all twenty senses, forty. Animals know there are a lot more senses than we humans consider in the sometimes flat language of words.

Hank and I are both solitary right now. Hank seems perfectly content. He helps me see that maybe I need this time touching down alone to fully sense and be and embrace who I am. We solitary birds can wholly engage our senses in the natural world around us, with no distraction. It's from this place, perhaps, that art emerges. Art—and maybe love, I wonder?

My marriage, I think, may well have been undone by "talk"

and abstract "ideas" that undermined our natural attraction and affinity. We'd have done better if we hadn't had so many concepts to disagree about. Maybe we humans would do well to be together more quietly, the way birds are, sensing each other, simply being together. For now, newly alone, watching and learning from Hank, I'm touching down fully within the sensory world. And Hank strongly suggests I lighten up so maybe I can fly.

> Tired of people who come with words, but no speech
> I made my way to the snow-covered island.
> The wild does not have words.
> The pages free of handwriting stretched out on all sides!
> I come across the tracks of reindeer in the snow.
> Speech but no words.
>
> —TOMAS TRANSTRÖMER

ANYWHERE YOU TRAVEL, fully touch down. Take in what the natural world has to offer with body, soul, and spirit. Get to the heart of each place. It will offer blessings if you ask. Wander to the center of town. Eat at a central café. Read local news. Learn songs and words of a new language. Talk to people in a park or pub. Find out what trees, flowers, plants thrive there. Explore land at the edges. Watch the birds. Open to animal sensing. Find a perch by water and be there, senses open.

Let your feet, skin, eyes, ears, nose absorb where you are, along with all the other senses you can't name. What sense do you experience that isn't among the normal five or six? Give it a name and then describe it. Do this in wild nature, if you can.

Find an animal or tree and pay attention to it. Take time to contemplate or notice in a deep way. Imagine that this animal or tree or flower is speaking to you. Allow yourself to take everything in. Remember or write down what message it seems to have for you. Allow it to become a poem or small gathering of words.

On a rocky island back at Chico Creek, I sometimes shift rocks to make a little bed and lie on my back on sun-warmed rocks, flinging poky stones into the creek—touching down fully with every part of my body and mind, watching damselflies and dragonflies circle above, allowing the heart of the creek world to soothe and enter all my senses, rushing away the busy human scramble. Often there's a blue heron just up- or downstream.

Go barefoot when you can and feel the energy of earth rising through your feet. Take off your shoes and walk on various surfaces—grass, concrete, dirt. Describe what you feel in writing.

Lighten up. It's all temporary, anyway. Mountaintops were under the sea. Don't hole yourself up inside or brick yourself in. The world might flood. Be ready to touch down somewhere new and live in another realm. Make sure there are birds.

> Watch any plant or animal and let it teach you
> acceptance of what is, surrender to the Now. Let it teach
> you being . . . how to live and how to die.
> —ECKHART TOLLE

7

daffodils and w-3

•

In truth, to attain to interior peace, one must be
willing to pass through the contrary to peace.
Such is the teaching of the sages.
—SWAMI BRAHMANANDA

Where is the lightning to lick you with its
tongue? Where is the madness with which
you should be cleansed?
—FRIEDRICH WILLHELM NIETZSCHE

Silvery bits of mirror flash along
the road in Upper Park near Turtle Beach. I glue them in a small
box, rearranging broken shards into a mosaic collage. A wood-
pecker taps nearby as I catch shifting bits of my reflection in scattered pieces, now a glimmering whole.

The year I turned twenty-one, I stopped looking in mirrors.

And for once in my life I stopped writing—catching my reflection—in my journal. After two winters struggling with depression, I had what's called a psychotic break. There seemed to be an edge like the drop-off in a lake when you're out on a sandbar and suddenly, at the next step, there's no bottom.

At Barnard College in New York City I got lost in the academic scene that surrounded my childhood. My journal, poems, ceramics didn't seem to matter. I thought I was supposed to do research in a huge city and write a B.A. thesis in anthropology. At the same time I was caught up in the so-called sexual revolution. Luckily, I avoided drugs.

I was deeply in love with a Columbia student named Joel, whom I'd met the spring before my senior year. My plans for life with Joel sank when he was drafted out of Peace Corps training in the fall and shipped off to the Vietnam War. New York winter days turned cold, dark, and short. Traffic sounds from Broadway rattled windows. Scratchy dust and globules like mercury gathered on windowsills. My senior thesis was due in the spring and I couldn't find a topic.

Caught in a downward swirl, I saw a psychiatrist near the spiraling Guggenheim Museum who never said a word, as I remember. In my dorm the winter before, also in a New York slump, I'd written in my journal, "There is a smallness in this room, and a lying self-importance and a paralysis and fear based on a misconception . . ."

I had myself cruelly pegged, but the awareness didn't help. I also wrote, "Sometimes the only way out is by going deeper in."

No longer writing in my journal by Christmas break in Chicago, I shifted from deep depression to psychosis. Panicky about my disjointed, delusional behavior, my parents took me to a psychiatrist, who said I must be committed immediately.

Committed? To what? I refused to go. Where? I was expected to pack. We must have included a gray skirt and gray sweater because, colorless, that's all I remember wearing.

Somehow I was transported to Ward 3 in Billings Hospital. W-3. I was convinced it was an out-of-the-way warehouse and I had to escape. Nothing was real. I remember a thoughtful, bearded doctor that first night who said, simply, "You're not as bad as you think you are." I think he could have helped me, but he left Chicago the next day. I refused to swallow pills and was held down and shot full of drugs. Later, blonde, cold nurse Kari made me drink liquid Thorazine and Stelazine in pleated cups of bitter orange juice.

Anything my mind could conjure up I turned against myself, my rampant creative practice. I even believed I was responsible for people dying in the hospital around me, my imaginative power of negativity was that great.

Every day my bundled-up parents trudged through snowdrifts of a historic blizzard to visit. Unable to help, they seemed pathetic to me. I turned everything upside down. Lovely Mom, pale and anxious, brought *Moby-Dick* and I insisted it was a fake edition. No book could possibly begin with the ridiculous sentence "Call me Ishmael." Mom became confused. Call me Ishmael? My handsome, playful father looked drained. He brought cartridges for my Parker fountain pen with a new brand name,

Quink. This was fake ink, I insisted, hah, Quink! Rattled, Poppa couldn't force the cartridge into place.

For once in my life I didn't need a pen. I was groggy with drugs and when I tried once to write in my journal, my words spiraled into black scribbles.

Eventually I learned to copy "normal" behavior and returned home in late March. The paranoia and dread gradually lifted. By late spring I was not only back to myself but felt clear, buoyant, and freer than ever before in my life.

I still wonder where it all began, genetics or brain chemistry or the middle of the night, in the ocean, in the womb, during birth, alone in a nursery, in a crib, calling for water, some profound moment of separation, the moment I began to sense I wasn't enough; I was bad, and it took an effort to "be good." I had to prove something for my existence to be valid. Simply being alive like a yellow spring flower pushing through earth was no longer enough.

Maybe I needed to go that far down to shake off mistaken ideas of who I was—other peoples', my own, or the notions of generations of intense Jews. I needed to learn that I can't always trust my mind, and that thinking can lead me in tight circles farther and farther from my heart. Far enough to be deemed insane. I learned I could free-fall out of myself. I could fail everyone, go to the darkest place locked-up crazy, watching my mind flit from one disaster to the next, and finally wind down, discovering in the emptiness that days were growing longer. Spring was coming. Daffodils were up from their own darkness. The world was turning without my help. My body was breathing for me.

The bearded doctor was right, I wasn't as bad as I thought.

I couldn't bring the world to a halt, only myself. Hmm. Earth still here, holding me up. Sun still here. Night. Rain on the way. Thunder. Sky. Stars. Fireflies. Reminding me to just breathe and shine and, yes, quit trying. Fall back. Eyes shut. Begin, in the quiet, to discover and simply be the creature you are.

Whatever took me to W-3 still tinges some mornings with dread. Even now I might wake up in the early morning disoriented and panicky. I can lie there obsessing about my family, how I might have helped my marriage, wondering if it's true that those of us who feel abandoned will likely abandon what we love—as I heard from a psychologist once. If I dive into the feeling and watch where it's centered in my body, it usually dissipates soon. Yoga shifts moods. And I'm helped by time spent in nature and on my various creative practices. Otto Rank, a colleague of Sigmund Freud, thought neurosis was "personality denying its own will." The only way out, he wrote, was through creativity. In his book *Art and Artist*, Rank suggested that neurosis was not an illness but the result of artists not creating.

Soon after my breakdown, I decided to pursue art and began working seriously in clay with my mentor, Ruth Duckworth. I loved making containers, especially bowls, as thin as I could spin, pinch, or slab them—as fragile and tough as I am. I found it grounded me to use my hands and body to make hollow vessels, some closed containers with a hidden center, egg-like, womb-like, cocoon-like.

When their Indiana Dunes house was sold the year before he died, Poppa told me why he had planted hundreds of daffodils there. A psychiatrist friend had told my parents I'd be better by

spring, "when the daffodils bloom." My breakdown was so ex-
treme that the doctor had correctly surmised it was a one-time
episode. The dunes house is still surrounded by Poppa's sloping
beds of daffodils. And I'm still more or less sane.

According to Daniel Matt in *The Essential Kabbalah*, sometimes a person can't comprehend his or her true nature "unless he
is completely shattered and then repaired through desire to return
to the limitless source." Now I'm grateful that my body, mind,
heart, and spirit shut down on a life I couldn't live, on work I
couldn't do, over the loss of my love to a war I couldn't bear, on a
way I couldn't be no matter how I tried. It's as if my soul called for
an internal meltdown, a small death, with me spiral-fizzing out of
control like a balloon let go.

All my life, I now feel in my body, down into my feet, I've
been preparing, taking notes, living to write and speak about all
this. To be this, whatever. A little wild. A little sloppy. Yes, out of
bounds. A little crazy. No holds barred.

> My barn having burned to the ground,
> I can now see the moon.
> —JAPANESE PROVERB

> If you express what is inside you, what is inside you
> will save you. If you don't express what is inside you,
> what is inside you can kill you.
> —GOSPEL OF SAINT THOMAS

8

one-mile moon
and blaubeuren

·

We need experiences larger than our problems.
We need to see we're wearing
the ruby slippers all the time.
——RICHARD BARTLETT

When I traveled to southern
Germany years ago to visit my grandmother's ancestral village, I
went to nearby Blaubeuren to see a body of water called the Blautopf, which is said to be bottomless. The entrancing pond-like
spring is piercingly indigo, the color of the sky just as stars come
out in summer. Divers who swim down to explore are reported to
disappear forever. According to legend, the *schöne Lau,* a beautiful
sirenlike mermaid, sometimes surfaces and lures people into her
watery home. The Blautopf (translated "blue top") is technically a

"karst" spring that opens into channels and tunnels that scientists explain using diagrams of the caverns and curves that eventually meet with the River Danube, which then runs into the sea. The Blautopf may well be bottomless.

I remember looking into the dizzying water wondering where the Blautopf begins and ends. Some days the world seems flat and I can't begin to see past the surface of things. On other days, sky, water, sounds, and people help remind me to look past appearances to the bottomlessness of everything and everyone. Staring into the small, bounded surface of the Blautopf and contemplating the unlimited nature of things, boundlessness and timelessness both within and without, somehow shocked me into an awareness of the opposite—the infinite held within the apparent banks of a small pool, the fleeting one-of-a-kind beauty of the moment, my one glimpse into this mysterious body of water in the present that's also infinite. Always now.

This evening I'm lounging in the creek at One-Mile in Lower Park under an August moon that looks like a moth's white wing in a spider's web. I'm sitting in shallow midstream current with a black-and-white dress shimmering around my feet. Above me, giant oaks gesture like animated statues under the moon's spell. Everything seems surreal, as aslant and wild as a visit to a spring with no bottom. I'm in a Blaubeuren mood. A toddler in a yellow helmet pedals an orange-wheeled Blazer. He's a weaving, bee-like satellite orbiting his jogging mother. A black Labrador laps up creek in the dusk, quiet except for the loud moon—wild albino wing in sea-blue sky.

Soon I'm home, waiting for sleep on the upstairs balcony under stars like a photo of fireflies. Jupiter's bright. I hide him under my thumb as a falling star flashes by—slash—as if to defy the planet and lesser stars. For a moment the sky looks like a vast Blautopf, and I'm almost afraid I'll tumble in, lose all sense of what's up and what's down and float off into timelessness. One star drifts. A satellite, I decide, and wave as it disappears like a night gnat over the roof of the house.

> We cannot live in a world that is interpreted for us by
> others. An interpreted world is not a hope.
> Part of the terror is to take back our own listening. To
> use our own voice. To see our own light.
> —HILDEGARD VON BINGEN

AT THE SUBATOMIC LEVEL everything is composed of photons, movement, and light. The Blautopf in Blaubeuren, like the mysterious photon (and whatever might be even smaller) represents to me all the potential of the unexplored self. Maybe some of us need to dive into the depths of self, no matter how dangerous it seems, to uncover more meaning, passion, expression of soul, and, indeed, more light. We might feel most alive in the presence of what seems most dark within us. There are many ways for us to begin to plumb our unknown depths and free our creativity without going crazy. To honor our boundless nature, it helps to shift perspectives and turn ourselves inside out and upside down.

If you can, stand on your head outside. Or, in soft surroundings, spin until you're dizzy. Try walking backward. A friend of mine walks backward up hills near his home. (The Chinese believe this is one secret to longevity.) In my journal I remind myself to sleep when I can under shifting stars and take what I call a "depth sounding" of each place I visit. Do whatever I can that rushes me to another place. Van Gogh rigged a hat with candles to paint *Starry Night*. Dr. Richard Bartlett, founder of Matrix Energetics, suggests we notice whatever's different in any situation and allow this to spread. We need an opening that allows us to see differently. Sometimes we need to create chaos to alter our frame of reference and allow for new information and new outcomes.

When he was three or four, my son, Dan, loved to set out in our backyard in Turlock on what we called "candle walks." From the back kitchen window I'd watch the small circle of candlelight around Dan bobbing slowly about the yard, stopping here and there like a moth. I don't know what Dan was experiencing, what he was illuminating, what he may have been burning. But I'm glad we let him do it.

Take a candle walk. Write in sleep or sitting in the middle of a creek. Go to wild places and invite the unexpected. Gather what you want onto a page or into a small box and allow yourself to sense the mystery in whatever is around you. Travel as much as you can, even within your own yard or town. Spend time contemplating water. There are many activities that can jog our brains and hearts and help us tap hidden tunnels leading to bottomlessness. Inviting playfully expansive "craziness" as well as regular depth soundings in our lives might help us stay more deeply sane, in touch with the ongoing present moment and with our true boundless and timeless natures, where the depth we seek is simply waiting to be perceived. Now.

> Creativity exists in the present moment.
> You can't find it anywhere else.
> —NATALIE GOLDBERG

9

....

oasis

·

The personal life deeply lived always expands
into truths beyond itself.
—ANAÏS NIN

When I was twenty-two, I read
one or two volumes of writer Anaïs Nin's recently published
(now-famous) diaries documenting the inner life and consciousness of a writer. She wrote, "For many days I lived without my
drug, my secret vice, my diary. And then I found this: I could not
bear the loneliness. . . . Joy was not necessarily in the south of
France, mystery in Morocco, art of storytelling in Haiti only. . . .
but might spring from one's own self. I shall have to create it from
within."

Nin became a hero to me and I mustered the courage to write
to her about the journal I had begun when I was fourteen. I sent a
short story about my recent breakdown, called "Oceans Remained." Nin wrote a loving, encouraging letter back and noted,

"Your journey will be like mine, from inner to outer and then unit-
ing them. . . . I hope you keep your journal for the 'sanctuary' and
flower outwardly. . . . One thing I assure you, I am happy and fulfilled in every way. It is possible to create a world even in this dark
one—a world of love and creation."

I learned later that Anaïs Nin responded to everyone who
wrote to her. I began to admire and respect her even more for her
generosity of spirit. I accepted her advice to keep my journal "for
the sanctuary." I was working at the time as a "blurb" writer, turning out jacket and catalog copy on subjects ranging from blister bee-
tles to biography. I've had other writing and journalism jobs since,
but always my true writing seemed to come forth in my journal.

I love the safety, smallness, and containment of it, the knowledge that I can write, draw, paint, tape, sing into it, catch things—
and in this way, let them go. For me, sitting in nature scanning
the world for what to tape or write into my journal is a form of
meditation.

I consult the journal as if it were an oracle, an entity, a water
hole, an oasis where the answers bubble forth when I hold it in my
hands and gather myself together on its smooth white paper. Entering the expansive world of my journal is my true creative practice.

My journal is my centering place; I slip into a quiet world
where I zero in on what's within and around me. It's a wide, pri-
vate, empty canvas to carry everywhere, welcoming possibility. In
the shelter of its covers I form, shape, hold, and dabble with who I
am. I've been tracking my life, working things over and out, writing poems, making lists, taping things down, and scribbling with
black ink since I was fourteen.

Just taking my journal into my hands, I breathe more deeply and feel myself relax into my body. In times of challenge, writing in my journal slows my spinning mind. In *Loving What Is*, Byron Katie writes, "The mind can be stopped through the act of writing. Once the mind is stopped on paper, thoughts can remain stable."

My journal helps draw the mystery of what's around me deeper in; it holds me and my sometimes dangling life together. We can weather practically anything with each other, Magic tape, and the right pen.

The future is not some place we're going, but one we
are creating. The paths are not to be found, but made.
And the activity of making them changes both the maker
and their destination.

—JOHN SCHAAR

10

....

on asking

.

If your nerve deny you, go above your nerve.
—EMILY DICKINSON

Questions are the keys that unlock the treasures
of creation. . . . And the questions
always hold the answers.
—EMMA SNOW (Purple Horse Woman)

If I ask myself what led me to write this book, I travel back in time to Turlock, California, where, pregnant with my second child, I sat in a crowd jotting the words of a dynamic young poet named Mike Engelbert into my journal. When he mentioned a writing group that fostered his poems, I felt strongly that I needed to be part of it. Did I dare ask?

I gathered up the courage to question Mike about the group. He sent me to meet Alice, who had started the small writing circle. I showed her my short story called "The Tunnel Woman," which had been triggered by a news article on men living in tunnels below New York City. My heroine fashions a den with scarves and candles and gives birth to her child alone in the tunnels. Maybe because I was pregnant and seemed vulnerable and liable to disappear underground, motherly Alice invited me to visit. I soon joined the group and six or seven of us met weekly.

When Mike moved away, we named ourselves The Bag Ladies after the Tunnel Woman story. A year later the group planned a reading at Cal State Stanislaus. I insisted it was impossible for me to participate. I dreamed about being pushed on stage in a leather miniskirt. I described how I had gone blank with fear all through my school years, rarely speaking in class, and freezing at a podium when I was thirteen, unable to remember my Sunday-school confirmation speech.

Somehow my friends talked me into participating, assuring me that I didn't have to be in the spotlight for long. After days of jangly nerves, I agreed. I began by reading parts of my long, new poem called "Open the Window," standing on my son's bathroom bench to reach the podium. I felt like the Jolly Green Giant, high as a tree. I found that I loved the microphone. I bonded with the audience and my friends practically had to drag me from my perch. Could this be my calling?

Soon a woman from California Poets in the Schools visited from San Francisco wishing to bring more rural areas into the program and invited us to train with her. Again I insisted there was no way I could participate. Sure enough, I was talked into training, nearly paralyzed with anxiety and awed by my friends' ease with schoolkids. I was convinced I could never do that. Linda, I

·

remember, used cars to add detail to writing, the way my friends
Maxima Putnam Kahn and Molly Fisk did once in a workshop
called "It's not a car, it's a blue Camaro up on blocks in the
driveway."

Terrified in my practice session in front of the group, I asked
myself how I might cope. Aha, kids love animals. I asked the kids
to write as an animal, even a roly-poly, or pill bug. There were
eagles, horses, jaguars, anteaters, emus, and parrots. The wild-
animal world rescued me. I was winging it.

I not only ended up with ten sessions in a classroom alone—
knowing nothing and panicky—but soon I became area coordi-
nator because no one else was free. And I eventually learned that
leading writing and creativity workshops was something I loved
to do.

Involvement with Poets in the Schools transformed my life.
I found my true family of oddball peers. At the first so-called
conference I attended, in the woods outside Willits, area coordi-
nators were asked to give a breakdown of activities. Bob Flanagan
from L.A. grabbed his guitar, collapsed onto his back on the
floor, and sang, Frank Zappa–style: Area breakdowwwwwn.
Area breakkkkkk dowwwnnnn! Hooray! I was home.

My new world emerged from that one poetry reading I attended in Turlock, at which I followed an impulse and asked for
what I wanted. I sensed it was vitally important for me to be part
of that writing group, and that I couldn't create what I needed by
myself; I needed a creative group collaboration, although I had no
idea why. I almost didn't ask, and once I joined, I was pulled

along, protesting all the way that I wasn't qualified. I'm still certain I'm not qualified. I doubt I ever will be. Maybe when we're qualified we don't have much to learn—or to offer. A Yogi Tea tea bag message reminds me, "Where there's mastery, there's no mystery."

For me at that time, asking had to be for something small and seemingly insignificant: an okay to attend *one* meeting of a writers' workshop. I never would have asked to join California Poets in the Schools, even if I'd known it existed. I was nearly overcome with insecurity. I had no sense of self-worth. I didn't believe I was capable of or ready for such a large step. I've seen since how the smallest step can set what we need in motion.

I wonder if our creative calling is sometimes something we fear, avoid, and, if we're lucky, end up being pulled into in spite of ourselves. If we follow our hunches, those little flashes of intuition, ask within, and listen to ourselves patiently, maybe it can be easier.

One slight move, a question, an asking, can lead to tunneling in, under, and through to where the seed of the creative rests lodged against the germ (or slug!) of fear. Somehow they grow together, informing each other. I wonder if the darkness of fear and limitation within us can be transmuted by the bright light of asking—inner and outer inquiry.

Regardless! My one small request in Turlock that night tumbled me to beginning what I most love to do.

I have found that you have only to take that one step
toward the gods, and they will then take ten steps

> toward you. That step, the heroic first step of the
> journey, is out of, or over the edge of, your boundaries,
> and it often must be taken before you know that you will
> be supported.
> —JOSEPH CAMPBELL

I WONDER IF ASKING, inside and out, may well be at the heart of a creative way of being in the world. After forming the right questions, we step up with our request. Will you travel with me? May I work with you? Would you be willing to . . . whatever you need. In my journal once I wrote after meditating, just as I was about to begin making collage boxes, "Bless and ask as you go, ask and bless." You might want to look at David Spangler's book *Blessing*.

We want to make our asking as large and world-opening as possible. Tony Robbins suggests we ask ourselves five life-expanding questions every day, generating more powerful answers. Visionary activist Caroline Casey advises that we ask with the words *I wonder*. Just out the back door, in that compacted, shady space where we're convinced nothing will take root, we might ask, "I wonder what will grow here." The words *I wonder* seem to open the way for a solution or at least a possibility.

I wonder how I'll make this a viable chapter. I wonder how I'll ever wake up. I wonder how I'll come to truly understand that our individual world is our place to create, dream, conjure, heal, plant, grow, and be. I wonder how I'll learn to ask more often and open myself to receive. I wonder how I'll cope with Poppa's dying.

Write several lines beginning with the words *I wonder*. Are there some closed-off areas in your life that might be opened with these words? Play with the words *I wonder* in your business, your daily life, and your writing. I wish, I dream, I imagine. Notice what happens when you begin to quietly ask within and without. See how your world deepens, and allow what you need and dream to come forth.

11

poppa's owl

Go deeper than love, for the soul has greater
depths, love is like the grass, but the heart is deep
wild rock molten, yet dense and permanent
—D. H. LAWRENCE

Yesterday before dawn, aware
Poppa was dying, I sped to the Sacramento airport on the way to
Chicago in the dark, clear cold. I didn't know Poppa had already
died. Out of starry night an owl, large, white, swooped toward my
car, seeming to spiral in a flurry just above my windshield in a tor-
nado of feathers. That's when I felt the emptiness. A low cloud
loomed in the south. I rushed into a sea of fog, suspended out of
the world.

Now my heart feels rushed open the way it felt when my
children were born. I wasn't expecting this shock of love. No
longer pent up in misunderstanding, it feels like a force penetrat-

ing the veils. Maybe that's what's most hidden in death, this loosening of love.

"The heart is a threshold," I wrote last night, "portal of love, portal of grief. Poppa's dead and the heart is letting this truth spread to the throat and wide to the edges of me, out and down and up, seeking him. No longer white, my heart is pink now, flopping a bit, moving sideways and stretching. It spills out like a river into an ocean and I know it will find him." I take my pulse in my wrist with my thumb. The force of heartbeat is palpable in veins throughout my body. Steady. How do you manage this, heart? I'm so erratic and you're so regular and true. Where do you come from, sweetheart?

Heart failure, Doctor Beauregard explained once, would finally kill Poppa after years of illness. Heart failure, my brother John said, is what finally gets everyone. John sketched the chambers of the heart into my journal: the atrium, the ventricle, and the arteries, a closed loop that's supposed to be a one-way flow. Poppa's weak mitral valve made the flow push back, confused.

In Chicago I wanted to fill the house, empty of Poppa, with candles. The first day I could find only the dinky food-warmer kind, so I set them in low bowls and the wax melted in little metal disks, pooled and hot like our hearts. They rested on the dining table with Poppa's stones, fluorite, quartz, a thunder egg like a dark cumulus cloud waiting to be split by lightning. My brother John and I bought a seven-day memorial Yahrzeit light and kindled it near sundown. We also bought daffodils, Poppa's flower.

In Chicago that night I wrote, "It takes a spiraling motion to reach him, clockwise, a vortex. I think the heart sends love in such a spiral. Hate's spin is tighter and swings back in like a spring with sharp points, but the love spiral softens as it opens to join all it encounters, sky, earth, water. It contains them all, and rock."

I write this on the bed, field-of-flowers pillow against my chest to cushion my heart that seems to be pulsing out through my arms and feet. It's nearly three days now, the time American Indians say it takes the spirit to fully leave the body. And the owl in many native cultures, I learn later, is a bird of transition flying between the realms. I felt my father's death take place within a larger heart, encompassing mine, flowing in and out of it.

Poppa explored the composition of earth and her sister planets—holding trees, oceans, the night where masses of fiery light spin, swing, spiral, and turn. Yet, the greatest mystery, perhaps, is right here steadily pulsing inside each of us, sending out small salty rivers with a composition similar to oceans, emitting silent messages in electromagnetic waves.

> . . . the infinite rests concealed in the heart.
> —MAHADEVIYAKKA

12

....

poppa's rowboat

.

How could he know
that once again
he would be taken
so by love

that again he would row out
in the night
on the black lake
while even loons slept
over featherless loon chicks

so hard and long across
Stone Lake with clouds
and shrinking trees

waiting for lightning
to send a final current

into the boat
and each flashing fish

leaning back, reaching back
through water
waiting for the fall
into water
like love

—S.W.

13

....

creekside alchemy:
gathering beauty

·

God's comments are conveyed by the images
in the natural world.

—GEORGE KEITHLEY ON GALILEO

The days just after Poppa died,
my brother Richard, with black eyes, hair, and beard and a wiry
charisma and intensity, heaped Poppa's clothing collections on the
bed in my old room as if he were on a mission to free Mom, who
wandered about the house too dazed to object. Now I wonder why
we weren't sitting quietly and allowing grief to have its way.
Weeping. Instead, we got busy with Poppa's collections.

My younger brother John, a gentle-eyed Paul Simon look-
alike, chose Poppa's favorite tie clips, a scrimshaw ship, and the
coat of arms Poppa wore most often, along with two neckties

dotted with airplanes from among hundreds of others. "Julian was a dude," Mom said. "Every tie here was worn." Mom, with kind brown eyes, hair still mostly brown, is youthful, lively, and girlish, short and "full-figured." She doesn't want me to use the word *zaftig*. Ha, I've snuck it in. I imagined sewing Poppa's ties together in a multicolored mile-long ribbon to bundle up the overfull house and ship it away.

"I brought this from the office for you," Rich said later, reaching in his pocket for a small, octagonal mortar with pestle, which he set in my palm as if it were an alchemist's grinding stone. Rich kept another for himself. Naturally Poppa had more than one.

What Poppa couldn't collect, he photographed. When he was a teenager he hung out at airports, and his photos of hundreds of small planes were stashed in boxes in the basement near his collection of fossil ferns and trilobites. Now I wish I'd saved those small glossy photos of airplanes from the 1920s and '30s. I'd like to cut them out and glue them in a series of old airplane collages or cards to send. Fly them forth into the world in another form, honoring Poppa with silver wings. Spangled flight boxes.

I grew up in the midst of Poppa's collections of rocks and crystals that now surrounded our mourning candle on the table along with fruit, cakes, and daffodils. Nearby, cabinets held a pre-Columbian priest's head, villagers dancing in a circle, and a blind hunchback in another of Poppa's overflowing collections.

Poppa spent much of his life gathering what he found beautiful. And I think he would have agreed with Einstein and Kepler that the rightness of an idea might not be seen first in its correctness, but in its beauty. Collecting was a creative activity, almost an art form for Poppa. What's all this gathering about, I wonder?

Today I'm crouching and gathering at Turtle Beach by the winter-full creek in Upper Park after a spring rain. Everything looks washed and alive. I'm filling a long, flat box with everything small I can reach, all wet and shiny: forty-two things. What kind of weird creature, I wonder, is making this cluttered collage? Sifting through small pebbles as Chico Creek rushes past, playing with juxtaposition, I feel as if I'm engaged in a kind of primitive and almost unconscious creekside alchemy. I search for a way to contain, classify, make sense. These objects represent what's near me in the rocks right now. Collage box as time capsule or mini-natural history museum holding leaves frayed to lace, weathered pine-nut shell, a wedge of blue plastic, amber glass, a bug carapace, basalt pebbles.

Each piece—a study of color, texture, shape—has a tale to tell of where it's been: in a bottle, on a tree, in molten lava, in the sea. Together they tell stories about the nature of the universe. I suspect this is what Poppa, a geochemist, was up to when he was studying mineral and crystalline structures in a high-pressure lab with ominous warning signs on the door. Exploring the composition of earth and what he called "her sister planets," maybe he was plumbing the secrets of the universe and of beauty, the molecular source of it all, the creative code.

Maybe our inner seeing can be triggered by beautiful "clues" on the outside. In my sometimes mindless "making," maybe I want to go farther—imbue boxes, journals, photos, pots, what-ever I make with what it means to be human. Maybe I'm longing to pack all my gatherings of everything within arm's reach to cre-ate a container large enough for my father's spirit as well as my own, my children's, my brothers', my family's, all our meandering love concentrated here in this goofy cardboard box.

WHAT DO YOU COLLECT? What did you gather into your pockets or your room as a child? What was or is at the heart of your collect-ing? Why were you gathering things, lining them up? What are you gathering now?

Consider collecting words; they don't take up much room. I'm glad I saved some of Poppa's words, more important than fos-sils. A few months before he died, Poppa called and said, "I dreamed you were a bird and you wouldn't come down to me." I remember the way he said "down," with a hollow, bottomless ring. I gathered his words, and said, "I'll come down to you, Poppa. But you need the right call."

Question your collections. How many turtles or frogs can a person live with? Focus on something you collect. Teacups? Ar-range them in a way that appeals to you and capture them on film. Choose ten photos and make a collage. Put the collection into words that capture their essence and take up less space. Decipher the meaning of your collections in your life. Take a depth sound-ing. Shake out their messages to you. Turn them inside out and up-side down, and consider letting some of them go to make room for the new.

foolsgold

·

The universe is represented in every one of its particles.
Everything is made of hidden stuff.
The world globes itself in a drop of dew . . .
the doctrine of omnipresence is that God appears with
all his parts in every moss and cobweb.

—RALPH WALDO EMERSON

14

----

telephone kaddish

·

What if you slept?
And what if, in your sleep, you dreamed?
And what if in your dream,
you went to heaven and plucked a strange and
beautiful flower?
And what if, when you awoke,
you had the flower in your hand?
Ah, what then?

—SAMUEL TAYLOR COLERIDGE

By believing passionately in something that still
does not exist, we create it. The nonexistent is
what we have not sufficiently desired.

—NIKOS KAZANTZAKIS

All I can ever remember of the Aramaic Kaddish, the traditional Jewish ritual prayer for mourning, is the first line: *v'yit kadal, v'yit kadash, schmei rabah*. I don't have a copy of the prayer. Yet, back in Chico one week after Poppa died, I phone women friends to join me reciting the Kaddish. I want to create a farewell in the realm of ancient words, a ritual container to somehow celebrate Poppa as well as honor grief.

Not having the words doesn't worry me, and I resist phoning the local rabbi in the same way I resist being in the Jewish fold. I've been daydreaming the gathering, feeling the elusive word-chant reverberate through me and my friends in the calm confidence imparted by grief.

Kathleen arrives early with logs for a fire and kiwis. The phone rings and it's Poppa's first cousin, Harold, age eighty-three—my cousin once removed, he reminds me. I met him in Chicago years ago and remember his chatty family newsletter, "The Ganze Mishpocha" (Yiddish for "the whole clan"). His mother was my grandmother Nanny's sister.

Harold tells me that my mother's phone message about Julian's death was muddled. As family newscaster, he wants a report.

Yes, Julian died peacefully, I tell Harold. Mom was with him near the end. Ethel never faltered. She and Julian were together, fully, all the way. I don't tell Harold that Mom's legs gave out the night Poppa died and she couldn't walk. That Rich rolled her from the hospital in a wheelchair. And I don't tell Harold that I haven't seen her cry, that I don't know where the tears are going. I don't say Poppa's death has me feeling recklessly daring and alive, almost as if struck by a jolt of creative electricity.

What I do say, is, "Can you recite the Kaddish?" Harold says "Yes, *of course.*"

Julian was the renegade bright-star atheist scientist who fled the Jewish fold, not Harold, who offers to stay home from temple to speak the Kaddish into the phone later so I can repeat it to my gathering friends. He suggests I call back when I'm ready.

My house fills with women, flowers, and candles, a minyan (more than ten) dancing to the Gypsy Kings. We light candles as I say the Sabbath Baruch, or blessing. We stand in a circle around the table and I phone Harold.

Do you have yarmulkes? Harold asks. *Yarmulkes!?* (The Jewish skullcap, used for prayer, especially among men.) No, I answer, but should we cover our heads? Yes, Harold says, and waits as my friend Maeve scurries upstairs with me to gather Nanny's hats with drooping wide brims, fruit and bands and veils. Maeve, dressed like a gypsy nun with a paisley scarf looped around her head, is soon to enter a convent. I doubt Harold knows we're all women here and nothing about this gathering is "kosher." I choose a felt hat, perched and spangled, sewn with sequins. Friends wear sunbonnets, a Greek fisherman's cap, straw garden hats, and a beret. I leave Grandpapa Mitch's old felt fishing hat upstairs.

Gypsy queens in hats, we stand in a circle holding hands around the candles and suddenly here it is, the Kaddish coming through the phone through the heart of Cousin Harold to me for my father, my mother, my friends, and all our parents. Here are the words in Aramaic, all of them—*v'yit kadal v'yit kadash schmei rabah . . . v'yit barach v'yit abach v'yit paar v'yit romam v'yit nasai v'yit nagar*—in a lulling chant, a drone, as familiar and rocky as nature, leaves, creek, unintelligible and warbling, encircling our hearts.

Finally we sing *Oseh Shalom,* the closing of the Kaddish for Harold, Adeline, all the meshuganeh Kallises, Mom, Dad, me, my children, my friends, our parents, the *Ganze Mishpocha* mourning together through the mysterious telephone.

As I wander near the creek more than a year later, golden seeds tumble out of a sycamore globe I finger into feathery darts. I tuck some into a walnut cup, wishing I had a box, idly imagining my "finds" arranged as a collage inside. It seems natural that there's a Top tobacco box waiting for me at creek's edge, just the right size for my gatherings.

It probably verges on sacrilege to compare dreaming up an empty tobacco box to summoning the telephone Kaddish to mourn my father. But sacrilege was, in a sense, sacred to Poppa. Being objective and scientific, busting out of the Jewish fold, refusing limitations and what he'd call ignorant superstitions of organized religion were vital to him.

Both the Kaddish and now the box help me hold myself together. No matter that calling forth the box seems trivial and the Kaddish meaningful, grand; one allows me to hold leaves and seeds, the other to channel grief in a prayer sent out through communal ritual. Both help me see that the universe will supply me with whatever I need.

The Kaddish is in itself a ritual container for spirit, a chant sent into the universe to invoke holy presence, a bridge or passage to my father in Aramaic, the pre-Christian language of spirit, with the passion and wildness of primitive utterance, holiness conjured to help Poppa leave in a rush of love. Wireless. Cordless. Wild and invisible. As golden as sycamore sheaths. Flooding the universe and each one of us.

WE NEED TO CREATE A SPACE within ourselves where a ritual can arise for dealing with pain and tragedy. Think about creating a ceremony to help you listen deeply in your life right now. Gather friends or family to do this with you if you'd like. Is there a passage you want to honor or celebrate for you or a loved one? Is there a loss you've experienced that you haven't fully acknowledged? Write down what you have lost and then what you might have gained from the loss. Burn this or bury it. Think how you might allow yourself to begin to let go.

On a walk this evening, I stood with my back to a giant sycamore. I found myself asking, out loud, may the energy of the sycamore enter my being, my mother, my children. Earlier by the creek I called forth, again, out loud, what I'm grateful for in my life, and what I want to open the way for. I always add, "If it's in the highest good of all concerned."

When I can, I let the nature of calling forth be impersonal, simply a feeling, an assumption, maybe an image and a calm, mindless sense of knowing.

Rituals channel our life energy toward the light.

—LAO TZU

15

....

wrinkle nose

·

To be spontaneous is to be divine.
—DANIEL ODIER

My kids, my brothers, their families, and I have all gathered at Mom's house to prepare for Poppa's memorial service a month after he died. Some of us are writing talks.

My brother Richard, in charge, a bundle of energy, posture upright as a pine tree, emerges from the basement where he's been practicing. He's emcee. Mom's house is filled with azaleas, orchids, daylilies, chrysanthemums. Traditionally in Judaism, the month after a loved one dies the family, especially the widow or widower, "sits shiva," staying home, receiving friends and relatives, who bring flowers, food, and blessings. Mom has halfway been sitting shiva since Poppa died last month.

My laptop is plunked in the middle of the dining room table in the center of the hubbub created by a dozen people getting

ready. I'm writing down bits of what everyone says, which I sometimes do in my journal. I started this spying "journalism" when I
was thirteen, documenting Mom's nags word-for-word about
walking the dog and dropping crumbs in the kitchen along with
Poppa's tantrums, "for cri yi yi yi yi yi yi yi yi." My recording has
always been precise. I counted the predictable eight "yi"s. Taking
notes this way can soothe me, center me. All my life I've been writing my way through things. That's what I'm doing in this book.

John asks if I'm writing my talk. No, I say, I'm just writing.
It's one of the ways I deal with things, I say, recording them obses-
sively. I'm meshuganeh, I say. Not wanting to be alone with this
label, I add, We're all meshuganeh. To me this Yiddish word
means "lovingly crazy." Nuts in an understandable, embracing,
family kind of way.

I realize I don't have a talk. I'm going to say whatever I say,
creating on the spot. As the meshuganeh daughter, I can get away
with it. I've rationalized that what's important for me today is
speaking from the heart and not worrying about crafting and
shaping.

I told Rich last week that his recent e-mails were so short that
they bordered on curt. Rich, a lawyer, explains it's because he
can't type. I feel sad that Rich doesn't have this creative, freeing
tool so vital to me. What would I do if my fingers couldn't fly over
these keys? I love typing almost as fast as I think, willy-nilly. For
me, spontaneity sometimes requires speed. Thoughtlessness. Of
course, that's just the beginning. Spontaneity, a form of inno-
cence, I've learned, can dissipate into nothing without form to

catch it, like a box for gathering. Or like the beginning and ending parameters of a eulogy or memorial talk.

Which I don't seem to be creating. I do plan to read one of my last e-mails from Poppa written spontaneously in his goofiest voice. "This AM Maw went to the prant and flar sale by the Coop. I told her not to buy any pansissies, pewtonias, germaniums, daffydollies, sunfloppers, maggyrolds, gladohlias, christandthensomes, loolies, dieloolies, daysillies and rolledingods." Goldenrods! In the free form of e-mails, Poppa and I began to communicate shortly before he died in a playful heart-to-heart way we never managed in person or on the phone.

Now, as the house fills with flowers, especially daffydollies, my girl, Elisabeth, is off somewhere by herself. My younger brother, John, is pacing. He asks if his talk comes after Chuck Hedges on clarinet playing "There'll Never Be Another You," a song Poppa chose for Mom. I fight tears for all kinds of reasons. It helps to be typing this down nonstop, mindlessly. Scribe of the day.

As if for a wedding, Mom tentatively drifts downstairs like a short daylily in a silk golden robe that belonged to Poppa's mother, Nanny. When Mom reaches toward the table, the robe rips under her arm. "It's okay," I say, talking and typing all this compulsively, "in times of grief you're supposed to 'rent' your garments." My son, Dan, explains the verb is *rend,* past tense, *rent.* I find Poppa's old maroon college dictionary and read, "Rend, (poetic) To tear (clothes) from one's body in a frenzy."

Through all this, looking young, old, pretty, quiet, composed, and distracted all at once, Mom seems only vaguely present, floating about the house. We've shed no tears together. We've done no wailing or keening like the soulful women I saw a few years ago in the documentary *Latcho Drom*, which depicts the Roma (often known as Gypsies) in periods of mourning. These women chant and sing grief in an artful ongoing, ancient song, like a cord in a looping trail to hold everyone together, bind up loss and keep it in bounds. I long for something like this. Thanks to our culture's rush to make the body disappear, we never got to be with Poppa after he died. To allow our feelings to come forth fully. To express them, freely, spontaneously, in the moment.

Instead, all month Mom's been fretting about food. Will it be ostentatious if there's a full spread? "I was going to get one of those big fish," she said. "Then I decided, no, I don't want everybody standing around a fish." In the short time since my decisive father's death, Mom's becoming more firm in her own opinions.

Somehow we all get dressed and make it to the chapel on time. Again it seems like a wedding with flowers and candles, a wedding of farewell. I carry stacks of votive glasses and candles in a clinking canvas bag. We enter small, elegant Bond chapel, which is filling fast. Mom greets like a young-old bride draped in widow's black. Suddenly parched with thirst, I carry six paper cups filled with water to the front for the speakers and drink five of them.

Then it's time. I light candles before a huge spray of daffodils and yellow daysillies and forsythia. There's a breeze and the flames stray high to the left and the candles drip like stalagmites. "Sunny Side of the Street" echoes from Chuck Hedges's clarinet on the back balcony. With the music, Poppa's heart pours in and

weeping flutters up between Mom, Elisabeth, and me, subsiding as
my brother Rich, like a rabbi or priest in calm control, welcomes
and introduces us. Poppa's Welsh cohort Nick steps up, describing
Poppa's magnificently annoying behavior in Cowboy Pool. He
mimics Poppa's two joke accents—Russian Greek and Jewish
Cherokee, he says. Next John speaks and then Rich, both moving
and eloquent, and then me, rambling, as I realize too late my heart-
felt need was to say nothing. Sometimes spontaneity calls for silence.

I'm followed by Poppa's wordy colleagues who describe his
scientific alchemy—experiments by hand in gold vials—his yells
of "Hot dog!" when an experiment went well. His creative vision
in bringing together geology, meteorology, and related earth sciences in the first geophysical sciences building, a new model of
collaboration. This is all too long and we're drifting.

That is, until my daughter, Elisabeth, Bopper, takes the
podium and creates the form of tribute we need, expressing feelings from the heart. (If only we wrote such things to the people we
love before they die!) Elisabeth reads notes jotted on the spot this
morning and last night, unexpected, fresh, and spontaneous yet
shaped into form, connecting our hearts with Poppa one last time.

She asks,

Did Grandpa know that we loved and feared him in a way
that is usually reserved for gods or superheroes? Did he
know that we dropped large objects down the laundry chute
with the eager apprehension of naughty schoolchildren? It
was only fun because we knew how loud Grandpa could
yell. . . . We also knew how loud Grandpa could laugh.

. . . When I think of Grandpa Julian, I think of crinoid hunts at the dunes, I think of hugs interrupted by beeping hearing aids, I think of woodpeckers, rocks, rhyming birthday cards, slide shows, and Mel Brooks. I think of the smell of wool and fresh air. I think of bushy eyebrows, warm hands, marbles, garage door openers, slightly rotten fruit, hummingbirds, corn shucking, my loose teeth, and shy good-nights from the doorway.

I always thought that along with my father, Grandpa was the smartest man who could ever possibly exist. He knew absolutely everything. I never heard a question he couldn't answer without complete certainty.

Grandpa called me Wrinkle Nose. A title created in honor of the crumpled face of my whining. A title I loved because it came from a man I loved so much. I don't know if Grandpa ever realized how huge he was to me, how important he was in my world. I'm so afraid he never realized the extent of his importance. I loved my grandpa Julian more than I even understand.

I hope he understood.

16

sweet surrender

•

"I just don't want to *be*," my mom confesses early one morning on the phone nearly two months after Poppa's death. She can't reach him. He seems far away now, completely gone, though it's startling to call Chicago and hear Poppa's voice echoing in ghost tones on the message machine when Mom doesn't answer. *Ethel and Julian would like to hear from you, after the beep.*

I convince Mom to fly to California for a visit. She arrives on the spring equinox and women of my co-housing village are gathering in a circle in our community building. Mom and I carry a candle and a sprig of rosemary with purple blossoms to add to a cloth altar next to someone's pair of white shorts to bring on spring.

Standing in a circle, we sing to the four directions, invoking the grandmothers. Sometimes I'm uncomfortable with what can seem like a self-conscious borrowing of Native American traditions, and I'm not sure my own grandmothers, Rosel and Cecelia, would like this at all. But tonight I'm delighted that my grieving mother's beside me turning north, south, east, west, invoking the grandmothers, disgruntled as they might be. *I call to you, call to you and see you smiling at me . . .*

Soon we pass a burning sage bundle to clear out the old and open the way for the new, singing a song I resist as schmaltzy New Age: "I'm opening up in sweet surrender to the luminous love light of the one." As the words are sung over and over, I enjoy the music pouring over and through me and Mom from our circle of women.

We take turns moving the smoking sage around each other, turning slowly to be "smudged," another Native American ritual, this one for purification. In spite of her shaky walking, Mom rotates with no hesitation to be smudged and then smudges me as I pivot beside her. She bends to my feet with the wand and wafts smoke up over my head to our voices, "opening up in sweet surrender . . ." Who could have imagined this?

I whisper to Mom that another song we're singing comes from the Jewish Kabbalistic tradition, "Return again, return again, return to the land of your soul." My grandmothers would have liked this one even less, I think. When I remind her we planned to stay for only a half hour so she could get to bed, Mom whispers, "I can always catch up on sleep." She's fascinated with our Northern California ways and wants to see what's next.

My neighbor Penny passes a tray of small earthenware pots, a kettle of soil, and four packets of seeds to symbolize what we wish to plant in our lives. Then we pass a talking stick and packets of seeds. Mom, just fourth in the circle, perched on a chair above us, says she only wants to watch. Holding the talking stick, she adds, "I want to tell you how beautiful you all look in the candle-light. I've never seen such a beautiful group of women." As I plant my tiny seed, I make the same wish I did last year: to live from my heart, trusting, fearless. Last year my nasturtiums flourished be-hind the house. This year I roast the forget-me-nots that shrivel in the western sun.

Our circle's large, more than twenty-five women. We sing a song to support each woman's wish, some playful tunes, like "I'm Gonna Wash That Man Right Outa My Hair," and some soulful, like "Amazing Grace." Most of us wish for peace, joy, abundance, openness. Ann, who lives just across from me, confesses she didn't know what I meant last year when I asked to live from the heart. Now she says she does.

One visitor wishes to be spontaneous like her kids, and Mom suggests we sing "I'm Forever Blowing Bubbles." Only Mom and I seem to know the words, "Pretty bubbles in the air." Nanny used to sing this to me with that mysterious face.

It's ten thirty, half past midnight in Chicago, when Mom and I stroll back through the co-housing village to my house on the path she names "the avenue." "If I hadn't been one of the first people to speak, I'd have made a wish and planted a seed," Mom admits. "What would you wish for?" I ask. "Peace of mind," she says with no hesitation. "It's not too late to wish," I insist, as we stand together under bright stars.

A few years ago I read that a twelve-hundred-year-old lotus seed from China germinated. I've always loved seeds. Seeds seem to me to be at the heart of the wild creativity in nature. They spiral, spin, swivel, float on fluff. They're barbed and they scissor, snare, stick, ferret, and burrow, holding life that's in limbo, sometimes within lush fruit. In Golden Gate Park one day years ago my kids gathered seeds from an Australian lilly pilly tree and we planted a few that never germinated. "Seeds are furious with enzymatic activity," says Barbara, a botanist friend of mine. (Enigmatic activity, I'm thinking.) To germinate they need a specific trigger, she explains, light, temperature, time, or water.

Poppa said his favorite seeds were the big ones, like the lotus seeds, with their long germination period. You can throw them at people, he said, especially avocado seeds. Poppa didn't like the light, floating seeds like dandelion and cottonwood: "They can sneak up on you and get you in the eye." Mom says she likes the seeds of black-eyed Susans because they made me.

After Mom heads back to Chicago, I send her some black-eyed Susan seeds from my garden to her garden. "Prant 'em," I write, in one of the mock accents that Poppa used. I'm not sure I added the words, "We've opened the way in sweet surrender. Now be sure to make your wish."

> This western paradise with its thousand and one
> nectared winds, this property of falling things
> which causes them to fly . . .
> —DAN WOOLDRIDGE

2

God's Mini-Storage

·

We tremble, thinking we're about to dissolve into
non-existence, but non-existence fears even more
that it might be given human form.

—RUMI

17

fellini:
on giving up

·

I know what the great cure is: it is to give up,
to relinquish, to surrender, so that
our little hearts may beat in unison
with the great heart of the world.
—HENRY MILLER

Floating in the tub this morning,
I realized that since Poppa died and with my divorce pending, all I
want to do is bask in warm water or wander near the creek alone.
For weeks nothing else seems possible to me. Writing, workshops,
meetings, traveling all sound pressured and exhausting.

Giving over to quiet floating, blank, letting go of what to do
in my life and all the dilemmas—after a time the floating itself begins to flood me with inspiration. The moment I forgive myself

for a long spell of doing nothing and let myself quit completely just to *be* (my heart's desire), I begin filling with stories about the heart, my family, my father, and here I am scrawl-writing this in the margins of a ripply magazine on the tub's edge.

One of my favorite movies is *8½* by Federico Fellini— known as *Il Mago,* the magician, in his native Italy. Marcello Mastroianni plays a famous film director in *8½* with a camera crew ready to roll and a large cast in full makeup and wild costume pacing around for days. The director can't come up with his movie. Finally, with actors rebelling, the despondent Mastroianni gives up. He calls a press conference to cancel the production. Newsmen arrive with cameras to record the scene.

As the director makes his announcement and the crew begins to disperse, Mastroianni's eyes gaze up. He raises his arms and spontaneously begins to direct his crazy (inner and outer) cast of clowns in a jubilant spiral up a tower to the oom-pahs of otherworldly music. The cast-away and suddenly reborn production begins with a flourish, Mastroianni himself joining in the dance-parade. The moment the director allowed himself to quit, to release his hold fully, the elusive movie vision came to him.

Sometimes when we give up and let go, everything's over. Other times, our work might just need time to incubate. I can't know whether I've dropped a project or it's just incubating. I think often, we have to let go fully, like the director, and accept not knowing. When I was writing *poemcrazy,* I got hopelessly stuck and dropped the book for months. Before long, ideas began to percolate in spite of me. When I began to write poems again for the pure joy of it, *poemcrazy* (called "Long Life Tea" at the time) opened itself up again, ready to go. I didn't know for sure that would happen.

By the creek just now, lost and stuck, I feel like dropping everything once again. What's the use? I tell myself. Why keep trying so hard? I decide to let myself give up on writing, on my life, or maybe to give it over. I find myself taking in a deep creek-fresh breath.

Listening to the water, I watch the creek and drift with it. I lie back in the grass with my feet in the water. A seed-laden stem curves over my face, dangling seven sheaves. A bird lands above a grapevine lifting into light. I call-whistle back and forth with her for a while. Floating, letting go, "out of my mind," I begin to notice what's around me.

To my right, a four-leaf clover nods patiently beside my hand. I sit up and idly flatten it into my journal. Hmm, maybe I'll call this "Lucky Beach." Heart-shaped three-leaf clovers surround me and I tape a few down. A mini-forest of intricate leaves appears within arm's reach—spindly, round, furry, ferny. I tape one of each in a random design. Everything begins to come alive the moment I allow myself to give up.

Suddenly I can't remember what's wrong. Clearly my life is blessed.

Come forth, *il mago*, inner magician, note taker, conjuring gatherer. Let the cameras roll.

> When the film is finished, it is never the film
> I said I wanted to make.
> —FEDERICO FELLINI

BUDDHIST TEACHER John Travis defines stages to the cycles in our lives: inspiration (or insight), action, satisfaction, and pause. In our culture, he says, we focus on "action" and slight the other three stages. When do you give yourself time for fresh inspiration? When do you need time to just rest in satisfaction after something has been completed? When could you allow yourself to give up, give over, or pause, and leave room for grace to slip in? The creative ocean of the unconscious may well be repelled by the pressure of "trying." When can you drop the ball and just be?

On New Dimensions Radio, David La Chapelle (author of *Navigating the Tides of Change*) said that something within us matches qualities in nature—sunsets and mountains. We need to retreat into nature often to find places where we can fully come alive. Like Poppa, La Chapelle's father was a geophysicist. He learned that all inventions come from invisible form. We must trust the emergence of these capacities from the deep structure of consciousness. First there's a disturbance in our world, says La Chapelle, a period of waiting, and then elevation when a gift emerges.

Visualization and affirmations often do injustice to truly tapping our depths, La Chapelle says, a profound process we don't want to cut short. The deeper the piece coming through, he says, the bigger the disturbance a person feels. I wonder what might have emerged if I could have had a long retreat in the natural world instead of being locked up and drugged on W-3.

The creative process is often forestalled because of discomfort. He suggests we tolerate disjointed disturbance to get to the gift coming through and go to a place of deep listening. Every being has a separate way of unfolding.

I learned . . . inspiration does not come like a bolt, nor
is it kinetic, energetic, striving, but it comes
to us slowly and quietly and all the time,
though we must regularly and every day
give it a little chance to start flowing,
prime it with a little solitude and idleness.

—BRENDA UELAND

18

damselflies emerging

·

The whole world is medicine. What is the self?

—Yun Men

All dizzying eyes, head just out of the husk, a damselfly's emerging at the edge of Chico Creek, like a mini-dragonfly with just one set of slanting wings. All bottomless brown eyes herself, Elisabeth spots another, smaller damselfly also inching its way free. With newly liberated front legs, it drags its compressed body from a black casing attached to a wide blade of grass.

Mom, visiting from Chicago, reads at a picnic table perched above in her pink shirt and straw hat, "fat and sassy," as she told a neighbor. Elisabeth's here from New York City, feeling lost after a breakup with her boyfriend of four years. She's lovely, slender, blonde, chic. Mom and I are short and dark, but we all share the same brown eyes, three generations of women, all experiencing loss.

Elisabeth and I are settled in a hollow beside a small fig tree surrounded by grapevines, letting the creek have its way with us, quieting our minds. The moment Elisabeth says, "There's a hole in my heart," the smaller twig-like damselfly flits onto her right knee in the sun, genuflects narrow window wings as if in greeting, and lifts off in perfect first flight. I flatten and tape the empty casing and blade of grass into my journal, next to slanting rows of little prayers I'm jotting down, a practice I remember when all else fails.

Finally free of the husk, the larger pale-green damselfly is a small stump slowly elongating, with wings expanding. "Things are drying out and unfurling," Elisabeth reports. "Those segments were round, now they're thin and cylindrical, turning golden brown," she says as we stare at the transformation taking place before our eyes. Woodpeckers rat-a-tat above, tapping a mini–drum roll to enhance the drama.

"Look," she says, "a blue one landed on me." Two more electric blue damselflies flutter by, mating in air, looking like a single, wide V-shaped creature. One's long tail end is curved to the back of another's head as if plugged into a bug brain socket at the base of an insect's version of skull.

Now Elisabeth notices a black pipevine caterpillar with orange spots hanging on a grapevine by a body thread over the creek in front of us. The caterpillar skin will split after the chrysalis develops inside. She points to other cocoons on the vine and many small husks. Our hollow by the fig tree is a breeding, cocooning, hatching spot. Shadows of emerged butterflies flutter past.

Elisabeth finds an empty praying mantis case. The mini-thread mantises have already squeezed out in this hotbed of creek-side alchemy we've come upon by chance. Years ago we watched

·

mantises extruding from a brown segmented case like filaments opening into skeletal mantis bodies with legs and wings.

My efforts at reassurance and cheer drift past Elisabeth, deflected by her almost palpable sadness. We hunker by the water and I toss more silent prayers into the creek, invoking the patient universe to open the way for healing. Soon we see we're in a living field of transformation, dissolution, dormancy, and rebirth, plunked down in the heart of a 3-D movie about cycles and solace.

Even my *unspoken* words to my daughter, "You're the emerging damselfly, the caterpillar hanging by a thread," ring hollow inside the living theater of creativity revealed in images before our eyes. Closely watching what's around us seems to lift us out of our convoluted inner dramas. I know that Elisabeth will soon enough be taking flight. I can see the glimmer of unfolding wings, but *she* can't. And I'm not so sure about myself.

I clamber up the bank to report on the scene to Mom, who can't walk well, much less climb. I describe the damselflies emerging. How radically their lives are changing. One minute they're encased in cramped darkness, the next minute they're free and flying. Bopper calls, "Mom, come quick!"

"Suddenly the big one flew off," she says. "It didn't move its wings even once before then." The golden damselfly flitters on the bank above as if waiting for me to admire it. Then I see its legs are stuck on a small burr where it's camouflaged. I guess even having wings doesn't guarantee flight. I free the damselfly gently with the tip of my pen and off it goes.

We three women seem to belong in this tangle of branches and vines where damselflies dart and light freely in front of us, a place of profusion and metamorphosis, where shifts take their own time, we see. Often someone or something (maybe the wind) comes along to give us a nudge, a little help. Sitting among abandoned husks and the molting insect casings that cling to strands and twigs, my daughter, Mom, and I have become part of this ongoing process, witnessing the transforming, creative nature of bodies, the world, and maybe even our hearts.

SITTING AND NOTICING IN NATURE can be an important time of gestation. Watch a damselfly or a bird simply being itself. It's important to have periods when we're not "producing" anything. We have to give ourselves space and time. Everything we need to inform our creativity is in nature. Paying attention in itself can bring about a transformation out of a small world of unhappiness into a larger one of discovery.

Every summer at creek's edge I watch tadpoles slowly develop frog legs, nymphs gradually become winged things over time. Speckly bits of quail egg shells hint at hidden hatchlings nearby preparing to fly.

We can't push cycles. Tadpoles become frogs whether they try to or not. Transformation is encoded in their cells. Sometimes they have to struggle against the current. Maybe this helps them develop strength. They become leapers. We, too, have to give ourselves space and time.

Let the natural world be your model. Notice the cycles. We can't rush grief or letting go. Finding our own way of being often involves risks we're hesitant to take. Notice how within the cycles of your own life, sometimes it takes your heart breaking before you realize what your heart may be asking you to do.

It's important to be heroic, ambitious, productive,
efficient, creative, and progressive, but these qualities
don't necessarily nurture soul. The soul has different
concerns, of equal value:
downtime for reflection, conversation, and reverie;
beauty that is captivating and pleasuring; relatedness to
the environs and to people;
and any animal's rhythm of rest and activity.

—THOMAS MOORE

19

freeing the creek

·

[Cultivate] willingness to be a fool.
—CHOGYAM TRUNGPA RINPOCHE

Today Elisabeth and I relax by the creek, enchanted, watching underwater caddisflies disguised as walking bits of wood like skinny living collages. Suddenly our peaceful world is invaded by a gang of teenagers slogging downstream fully clothed, hurling branches and logs to shore, turning our haven into a churning swamp. Birds flee as the crashing horde ravages the small dam of river stones, heaving rocks toward shore, falling backward, laughing. We stare aghast, like the audience at a shoot-em-up movie seeing a SWAT squad blast the hero's home asunder.

Paralyzed with righteous indignation, we watch nearly half the water drain out of our Sandy Beach swimming hole as the hooligan yahoos stagger downstream. The water level on our mermaid boulders across the creek sinks nearly a foot. How dare these flash-flood strangers mess with our wild creek!

Still stunned, Elisabeth begins to gather rocks to mend the dam when a woman across the creek waves her arms and calls out to us. Her youth group, she explains, is clearing the way for native salmon that swim upstream to spawn and are hindered by dams like this made for swimming holes. Oh my God. The rampaging hooligans are freeing the creek. We're the yahoos here, among the ignorant basking dammers. Chastened, we too begin tossing rocks away.

Now I'm wondering, just how often am I part of the problem, clogging things up, unable to see? Okay, universe, stop laughing. No. It can't be most of the time!

It can take courage for us to realize we've had the wrong idea and made wrong decisions and need to change midstream. We might be in the wrong city for us. The wrong relationship. The wrong life. Writing the wrong book. If we have to be right about everything, we won't allow ourselves to change, and to free our creative natures.

I'm slowly learning to allow myself to be wrong. When I was twenty, my nervous breakdown taught me how deeply wrong I could be. I was in the wrong school, in the wrong city, aiming myself in the wrong direction. I was wrong in my very understanding of my own nature, which I judged inadequate, damaged, ruinous, even. Usually when I realize I'm wrong, it's a great relief.

Yay, I'm wrong! Maybe the world isn't coming to an end after all. Maybe I haven't ruined my life. Maybe . . . And everything

I've been wrong about, and am still wrong about, undoubtedly, is most likely what I've needed to experience to wake me up to what *is* right for me.

Sometimes it hits me that I'm wrong about most things. About time. About my place in space. About the nature of the body. About the nature of the divine. About human nature. About what death is. About who I am and who my kids are. And about what the creek needs to support the salmon and all its visitors.

But heavens, let's not worry about being wrong! I'm gradually learning that, paradoxically, it's the foolsgold—the blunderings, giving ups, breakdowns, in spite ofs, chance encounters, shatterings, letting gos, and mess-ups—that has led to most of the creativity in my life, not the sweet making of something beautiful, or "enlightened" inspiration, and certainly not feeling in control. It's the opposites, listenings, buzz hums, the falling (leaping) down the rabbit hole, the stepping through the looking glass, barefoot, with no suitcase, in new territory.

Now an open channel flows through the middle of the broken dam at Sandy Beach, wide enough for a salmon—or person—who might want freedom to swim upstream in the creek or flow down. A yellow heart-shaped catalpa leaf spins past underwater. It angles itself like an arrow and shoots heart-point first through our newly hooligan opened channel into shallow rapids rushing toward the Sacramento River, the Carquinez Strait, and the Pacific Ocean, free as the creek.

WHAT DO YOU FEEL CERTAIN ABOUT in your life? Are you sure it's true? Read *Loving What Is* by Byron Katie, who suggests we question everything we think we're sure about, especially when it's a judgment. Our fixed ideas dam up creativity. We might need to be right more than we need to be creative and free. We can at least open to other views and ways.

What's your personal idea of freedom? Begin your excavations. What in your life, your body, your job, your business, your world, is dammed up that needs freeing? What beliefs or ideas or judgments have you been holding that might need to be released? It may well be ideas you feel sure about. A position you're proud to hold. You might want to write, "I believe [list five things] because . . ." Then assume the opposite and write (for all five), "I might be wrong, because . . ." Listen to yourself the next time you're pontificating on a soapbox. Listen to opposing viewpoints. Look at opposites. Seek a third way.

> The greatest discovery of my generation
> is that a human being can alter his life
> by altering his attitudes.
> —WILLIAM JAMES

20

always green inside

·

The river is within us.
—T. S. ELIOT

I'm sitting by the winter-full creek adding so much stuff to a small collage box that it looks like a mini–junk drawer in my kitchen. I glue a square of orange plastic near a black pebble, a blue twist tie, and green foil. The river-wide creek rushes by, empty and clear.

It's often difficult for me to know when to stop—talking, thinking, writing, gathering, gluing. The book you hold had hundreds of rambling, possible chapters. When a friend told me I don't need to include the kitchen sink, my response was to begin a chapter called "The Kitchen Sink." Luckily, most of what I come up with no one sees.

Juvenile halls are brimful of people who mess up, including me. This year I'm in a windowless but cozy room for an overfull workshop with all of the Butte County Juvenile Hall school's sixty-five salvage kids huddled around desks in mumbling groups of four. I experience an odd sense of safety here in time-out, with just over an hour to help these kids enter poem land, while hefty men cruise corridors with cell phones in holsters, like pistols, at their hips.

Most of the kids are scrubbed-looking boys in green or yellow T-shirts; no gang colors allowed in our culture's underage version of prison. A few kids are here for murder or rape. The girl who pulled a gun in her junior high class just left. Many kids are in the Hall because of drugs or petty theft. One kind of mess-up or another.

Luckily I don't know who did what. I call each kid sweet-heart. What other word will do?

I show them pages from the safe world of my journal, flat-tened wildflowers—scissor plant and butter-and-eggs—and the word *zigzag* clipped from litter. I'm free inside myself to create my idea of beauty or to mess up, I explain, with no one watching, and it keeps me alive. I hold up my Scotch tape and joke, "Maybe this is a weapon?" and learn that yes, it's contraband, along with the word *zigzag*, the name of a brand of cigarette paper. Even the pointy acorns in my pocket are considered dangerous in the Hall, land of the forbidden.

I read Francisco Alarcón's poem "Drought."

> despite
> dry
> years
>
> *siempre*
> *verde*
> inside

Always green inside.

The artist-teacher Luisa, who's Native American, exotic, pe-
tite, and lovely with long hair tied back, writes this poem high on
the board. Six words. That's what my journal means to me, I explain. It's an oasis to keep me green inside. We all need an oasis, I
say. Almost every kid copies down the words, *Despite dry years
siempre verde inside.*

We create a word pool on the board: *sizzle fizzle boozle.* I say
I like *z*'s and they keep popping up. We talk about opposites. Opposite of calm. Wired. Opposite of coma. Ecstatic. Opposite of creek.
Cement block. Opposite of thunder. Nap. Opposite of sky. There's
no right answer, I assure them. What a relief. They love playing
with opposites. I jot down words: *euphoric moon drizzle x-rated
anonymous ocean whisper swirl hypnotic coma lively sultry chronic.*

When we write about ourselves using gathered words, Jesse
begins. "I'm like the wind. I creep I pack I resist I run I get caught
I'm like a ball of fire that just can't be stopped. I draw what I
see . . . I'm like a camera on a Wednesday, gypsying in a river. . . ."

I love *gypsy* used as a verb, I say, reading aloud, *gypsying.*

Someone wants "pissed off" when I ask for feelings on the
board. I'm glad I can't be fired, I say. Luisa works, with good nature, to keep everything—especially me—in bounds. "Don't you
do anything," she tells them, fiercely, once, "to get locked up, to
jeopardize your freedom."

This is about freedom, I see. Including freedom to mess up?

Poems and freedom belong together. Yet on the "inside,"
I'm reminded, these kids must learn to "be appropriate," follow
the code, in order to live "outside." On the second day, Luisa and

I search for the word *gun* to remove from a poem. Many words are taboo in the Hall: *red blue diamond brick speed weed grass crystal snow,* to name a few.

The second day, the current White Pride neo-Nazi gang leader gives me his poem, about being a meth addict, in which he's an old man angel visiting his younger self, believing in that self and speaking as the voice of his conscience. The gang leader agrees that one day he might help troubled kids like him. This would come from his messing up. He writes poem after poem, even after he learns I'm Jewish. He wants to be in this book. His desire to express himself and be heard seems greater than dogma or duty.

There are other gang leaders here, Asian, black, Chicano, white, and I unwittingly read one leader's poem, "Window Warrior," which, in a code, ridicules another leader, "with a chasm above his brow." The poem causes a hubbub with reverberations. Ten kids are placed in lockup that night and miss class the third day. We're down to a mere fifty-five.

The next session I return to the Hall feeling embarrassed and upset. But strangely it seems almost as if I've passed an initiation. Messing up, I learn, brings me into the bosom of the staff, opposite of what I had expected. After all, this is a palace of screwups. All the staff makes mistakes sometime or another, I'm told. The kids screw up. Wow! Screw up and you belong. I seem more vulnerable now, a real person. I'm no longer "the writer" but "the human" at ground level. I feel relieved and accepted not for being perfect, as I try to be, but for messing up in ignorance.

The poet Rainer Maria Rilke wrote, "It is only our vulnerability that will save us." Maybe when we screw up we create an opening to connect us to others. Especially if we screw up and don't run away. Admit it. Try again.

When I took a Ropes Course program once, I was determined to do everything on my own. I climbed without help, balanced my way across a beam like a self-sufficient perfectionist, without slipping. But soon I learned that the less coordinated, brave people who had trouble and needed help led us to lift, hold, struggle, collaborate, unite, create a bridge, and begin to laugh and play as a team—and care about each other.

By the time my four days with these kids are up, I feel at home. I've told them I had a breakdown once, when I was twenty, just a bit older than they are, and I, too, was locked up against my will. For the time being, we're a confederacy of mess-ups. Creativity can be chaotic, and we're hungry to create.

Chaos means "the great becoming" to native peoples, I learn from Jane Middleton-Moz. Only in Western culture, she says, does *chaos* mean "disorder." In the chaos of becoming, we kids in the Hall don't have a lot to lose. We're wild to write poems. We've tumbled from a variety of pedestals early, freeing ourselves from expectations. We can create loosely, sloppily, with depth and mistakes and range and passion.

> Anyone who has never made a mistake has
> never tried anything new. . . . There is only
> one road to true human greatness:
> through the school of hard knocks.
> —ALBERT EINSTEIN

WHERE IN YOUR LIFE do you need to be perfect? In your dress, your writing, your work, your drawing, your parenting? Look for areas where you're especially demanding and hard on yourself. Take a day of sick leave. Let yourself mess up. Be sloppy. Play the fool. Do something wrong. Play hooky. Write about it. Break something. Put it back together in a new way. Even the great Picasso said, "Every act of creation is first of all an act of destruction." Make an ugly collage or drawing or poem. You may be surprised by the new wild beauty rushing in.

In Glenwood Camp Juvenile Detention Center I suggested kids write their rebellion rather than steal or kill or fill themselves with drugs. Excitement rose among this quiet, contained group. The large room almost lifted off the ground with their energy. They came to life with the refrain "Can't give you up."

Play with this refrain yourself: Can't give you up, road world, can't give you up, fast driving, can't give you up, wild heart madness. Can't give you up, spelling mistakes. Can't give you up, flying dreams, typhoon feelings.

It was an accident! It was an accident!

Everything I do is an accident!

—DAN WOOLDRIDGE, age three, in a flooring shop after

knocking over a row of carpet samples like dominoes

21

the language of red

·

> What about myself, then!
> What am I doing, bursting into paint?
> I am a writer, I ought to stick to ink.
> —D. H. LAWRENCE

A small tab of red cardboard litter from a walk along the creek this morning pops up in my mind as I drift toward sleep at midnight. I tucked the tab in my journal but tossed it out when I got home. Now it won't let me be. It belongs in my journal or a collage box. I'm gathering energy to roll out of bed and find it.

Instead I doze off remembering the day Dan ran up to me when he was three or four waving a painting. "Boo! Mama, Boo!" (blue), he said, "Wed, mama, Wed"! (red), thrilled with the colors and the discovery that he could spread them.

The word *red* wakes me enough that I go downstairs and rummage for the discarded tab. Tea bag label, soup container, crumpled paper. How could such a bright thing disappear? Wait a minute . . . aha! Here it is, stuck in a corner of the garbage bag, my vibrant dab of scarlet box top like a miniature hidden heart-color valentine.

Why is this scrap of red so nourishing to me? Normally I resist red. Now, after months of feeling I'm under water, I must need the remedy of red's heat, transgression, life. Shift. There's something about the red that warms me. When I concentrate on red I feel enlivened, embraced. It reminds me to close my eyes in sunlight and fill myself with healing orange-red. I can understand why Terry Tempest Williams wrote, "I want to learn how to speak the language of red." Slow down, it says, and at the same time fire up. It wants calm, centered passion. Spark. Beginnings. It's the first chakra revving up.

Furthermore, this red is the edge of something I see with my eyes shut—a long line of color at the tip of a brush urging: paint. Wait a minute. Paint? I freeze up when I paint. I'm afraid red wants to thaw that ice. Well, often I carry Austrian Cretacolor pencils. A dab of water turns them to paint and sometimes they spread timidly through my journal with a mind of their own. Pale blue. Ocher. Yellow.

The colors I need seem to shift. I craved yellow, I'm reminded, before red moved in. I bought yellow plates, napkins, pillows, a vase from Portugal, paint samples for my white walls. Yellow's message was simple but not easy: lighten up. Fill with sunlight. Be radiant, a beacon. Imbue even your writing with light.

Increasingly I understand painter Wassily Kandinsky's statement "Color is a power which directly influences the soul."

Lately I choose clothes like paints. The colors I wear both reflect and influence my moods. I might need a bit of green, or a warm, peachy scarf, set against black. I might seek out pink to warm me, and mother-of-pearl earrings with an iridescent wave of otherworldliness. It's early spring and I love the chartreuse of budding leaves and my filmy shirt that color.

Meanwhile, I've "borrowed" the red hat I once gave Mom. I bought a red dress, scarf, silk shawl. Maybe I'm unconsciously being the flower seeking to attract the bee. I'm eating beets, adding radish to cucumber salads, carrying apples, and filling up on red, turning pink.

Japanese sages, I've read, advise us to play at everything in life. Even dying. When I know I'm "only playing," I feel safe. To seers in India all the world is *lila,* a kind of divine game.

When Dan and Elisabeth were toddlers, I brought home large appliance boxes. Some hot summer days in the backyard they'd paint a big box, the grass, and each other with fat brushes and jars of powdery tempera colors. For the fun of it.

And now red, with its secret of unlimited energy, is bringing a full prism of colors my way. I want them to take me, lightly, wherever they want me to go.

SEE IF A COLOR CATCHES your eye on a walk. Buy paints or colored pencils that become watercolors. Tape color into your journal. Read *Spilling Open* by Sabrina Ward Harrison and see how she dashes color into her journal.

Pay attention to how colors trigger different aspects of creativity in you. Each color has an energetic frequency that affects us in its own way. Notice how color appears in nature. Aside from green, sky blue, earth brown, most colors appear only temporarily, in rainbows and sunsets, or in small things, flowers, bugs, and birds. I love the book title *Colors Insulting to Nature* by Cintra Wilson. Large garish billboards can seem like an insult on country roads.

Fill a box or any surface with many shades of one color. White on white. Sea green on forest green. My friend Joann and I took a walk in San Rafael one morning. Beginning with an abandoned scrunchy, she gathered blue for a box to make later. Blue for peace, sky, melancholy, tranquillity, infinity. I heard myself say to Joann that making these boxes allows me to have an artist's eye out in the world and brings me more alive in each place. We agreed that without the limitation of boxes, or some kind of framing containment, we can be overwhelmed by what's around us.

Yesterday on my patio, squishing blue and white acrylic onto a plywood board, I painted more than twenty small boxes. When they're blue, empty containers shift from match or jewel box into small sky or sea box, realm of heaven or ocean. Next, for fun, I painted everything glued in one box blue, a magic bouncing ball, a small Easter bird, an opening seed pod, and two squashed bottle caps.

In India there is a festival of colors called Holi. Hold your own inner or outer festival of color. Invite color into your dreams. When you wake up, paint or draw or cut out the colors you dream. One of my favorite painters, Odilon Redon, wrote, "With pastels I have recovered the hope of giving my dreams greater plasticity. . . . Colors contain a joy which relaxes me; besides, they sway me toward something different and new."

22

digging up the artemesia

·

We need, in love, to practice only this:
letting each other go. For holding on comes
easily; we do not need to learn it.
—RAINER MARIA RILKE

A billowing cloud of gray-green artemesia blocks the path from the front walk to the garden beside my house. I've been hacking with loppers and jamming the shovel underneath for two days in a feeble struggle to uproot it. I have pungent artemesia under my nails and in my pores. After several years this fierce, embattled sage is the diameter of a tractor tire.

I look a bit gray-green myself right now, moving toward my first Father's Day with no father this Sunday, the same week Kent and I sign divorce papers. I pulled a redbud sprout and a mini–liquid amber tree with ease at our old house earlier today when I took Kent the Marital Settlement Agreement, just notarized. It's his turn to sign. I turn on the hose. I've watered the asparagus fern outside the front door whenever I've picked up our dog, Emma, the whole time we've lived apart.

Drought-resistant, this artemesia needs very little watering. Its tenacious roots developed in just over three years. The marriage has been thirty. We've been uprooting the marriage while the artemesia has been growing roots toward Hong Kong. Maybe I need a jackhammer. My old ways hang on for dear life.

Ridiculous as it sounds, I dig up more of the artemesia every day. It's a complicated plant I love, tough yet delicate and lazy, with cascading featherlike seed flowers, silvery monotone like the ocean. Some roots tunnel just below the ground with a drape of root hair along with deeper fibrous roots and tough stems coming up like a forest alongside the central stem that won't budge. Maybe this is making me stronger, both the divorce and the digging. Maybe I need this battle right now. Or a bulldozer.

"Why do I mourn this waning marriage?" I ask myself in my journal. "It's been the structure of your whole adult life, Susan," I hear. "Allow yourself to grieve." Then, "How long can I wallow?" I ask. "As long as you need to, darling," I counsel myself. "Everyone else is living a regular life and my heart is broken," I write, and I'm informed within, "That's how it *seems,* dear."

The next day, after angling the spade inch by inch under the artemesia in cement-like dirt, it's time to wash my hands and go to the paralegal to sign divorce papers with Kent. I counsel myself to allow everything to change form. I enter what I call the larger place, blessing this transformation within my journal once again, ad infinitum, asking that it be in the highest good for all of us. Go quietly, with composure, my wiser voice tells me.

And wash your feet.

Another day has passed and I must confess this morning I bought a new small artemesia at the farmer's market. I resolve to put it in a better spot toward the edge of the garden. The man said it was an angel artemesia that will only be a small mound. An angel! I've been needing a lofty, light-hearted, easy-going angel.

I meet Kent at the paralegal's office and we sign the agreement. I tell Kent I'm not sure he's getting a good deal. When Kent assures me he's happy with the plan, the paralegal says, "Did I hear you two right?" She's used to discord. Our divorce will be final in six months, just after the new year. There's been no great drama between us. Our marriage just wore down over the years. Our fundamentally different temperaments led to misunderstanding and finally inability to live together. For whatever reason, I was never able to imagine us beyond our years with the kids.

Just the same, driving home, I'm weepy. A dead blue jay flashes iridescent on the roadside, head curled, bowed, like the grieving angel on a card Claudia sent when Poppa died. This elongated, chubby blue heart of feathers by the side of the road looks the way I feel. And it could probably do a better job of digging.

Now, more than a week later, hopeful green fingers inch out of the hacked-back stems of artemesia because, honest to God, though I dig a bit every day I still can't uproot the damn thing. The central core, stems, and roots hold out like a small, ravaged forest fighting for life. Poppa always told me that the life force is incredibly strong.

On the eve of Independence Day, Dan visits and digs up the artemesia for me. He hacks and chops and pulls dramatically, hoping to make me feel less incompetent, tearing out hairy roots reaching sideways several feet. Finally, wearing my old wooden clogs, jumping up and down on the spade, he twists and tugs and yanks out the last of the wily sage. Together we admire her persistence, her tenacity, and her roots.

And we've created a deep, loose, free open area where I can plant anything I want, maybe a pomegranate. And daffodils.

Later we dig a roomy hole for my new angel artemesia, a delicate silvery mound. As I pack the earth around its lively roots, the lacy winglike leaves seem to whisper reassuringly that new beginnings, new encounters, new creative awakenings are on the way. From the kitchen window I can see that angel now, glimmering beyond the back patio.

I TAPE A SPRIG OF THE OLD ARTEMESIA in my journal to hold its fragrance. When I collect things in my journal or in the boxes, I feel freer to let go in the outer world. That is, in my life! The journal and the boxes give me the illusion that I can keep from losing each day. I can catch little bits of evidence on a page or in a box, the beauty of a place. A person. A marriage. Well, at least a flower. Here's a petal, a kind of shorthand for the magnificence of the rose, one spring leaf, representing all of spring coming forth at Wisdom Beach. If I could gather some creek in the box, I would. Concentric rings of water. Ripples. My journal fell in the edge of the water last month and the creek is now rippling there in foggy, illegible words. And here's a bit of robin's egg, crushed under tape. Aha, maybe I've captured spring. And beauty.

Where do you need to let go in your life to make space for

something new? As mother, father, lover, wife, husband, friend, writer, artist? What the heck does this have to do with the creative process? Burrow to the heart of it. Think about how you might need to dig something up to create more space around you for your creative being.

Look for something in your life that's both super-fragile and tough, like the artemesia. Paradoxical. Like an egg. Like your heart. Breakable as hell, yet also resilient. Deeply rooted.

Make a collage or write a poem or story that holds things both fragile and tough. That frees you to dig something out that needs to go. Notice both the toughness and the fragility of what's around you. How do these things remind you of yourself and/or your relationships? What fragile part of you needs to do something hard? What do you resist releasing? It might be something within yourself. A habit, a fear, an idea, a belief. It might be a hairdo, a beard, a job, a person, a relationship, or something taking over in your garden. Write about it.

What do you need to break or risk uprooting in order to be whole? To create who you secretly know you're meant to be?

23

god's mini-storage

·

You cannot lose what really belongs to you,
even if you throw it away.

—*I Ching*

Mom says there's a blizzard in the Midwest, and I've forgotten my jacket. Enveloped in the Valley's first winter fog, I'm driving at dawn to the Sacramento airport en route to Chicago, where tomorrow Mom, my brothers, and I will scatter Poppa's ashes. To add to the Sturm und Drang, today just happens to be the exact day my divorce is final.

I don't know how we'll get Poppa's ashes through the ice in Lake Michigan, I told friends last night. Tanha offers to lend me her pick. I gathered friends to create a ceremony of blessing on the eve of my official divorce and the anniversary of Poppa's death. Ten women sat at my round table in candlelight, each with a silver sphere—crackled glass balls I bought on sale at Nantucket as "party favors." We wrote wishes and blessings for ourselves and each other on white ribbon to slip inside the spheres through a dime-size hole left for the glassblower's breath.

I opened Daniel Matt's *The Essential Kabbalah,* by chance, to "Shattering and Growth," and read about ten spheres of light, or sephirot, that grow like seeds and can't maintain their original form. While seeds must decompose before growth, these spheres of light can become perfect only by shattering.

Well, driving in the chilly morning, with my silver sphere intact at home, I'm heartened to know falling apart is just what I need to do to become whole. I guess flipping out wasn't enough, damnit. Still, I'm grateful I found the car key and my disappearing glasses, and that the car's clean and full of gas. For the most part everything's in place. Everything, I think to myself, except my jacket, a cozy form of shelter.

I feel more than a bit out in the cold since Poppa's death and my divorce. I got weepy just hearing a book title, *The Shelter of Each Other.* Wrapped in my skinny velvet scarf, I zoom past a sign that reads, "Bridal Show at Y & K Fairground," reminding me that for the first time in thirty years I can no longer say "my husband." I wonder how I'll find ways to see this as a blessing.

I remember telling Kent when we separated that I thought this divorce might be a big mistake. He said, "If it's a mistake, it's a mistake that's going to be made." Why do I find that reassuring? We can make mistakes. We do make mistakes. We go on from there.

Just before Grumpy's Kiwis for sale outside Gridley, I whiz past G&D mini-storage. Without thinking, I read G&D as God. It's sacrilege to say God's name or even write it in Jewish holy texts, so it's abbreviated, G-d. God's mini-storage. Where things begin to coalesce. A vast, mysterious shelter for everything. Would that include walnuts? Wings? Road signs? Trees, babies? Elephants, along with pianos? Marriages and divorces? Maybe everything in sight. Everything on earth. Within and without. My children. Kent. My father. My brothers, Mom, and me bumbling about in the Chicago snow with a clump of ashes.

I asked for Kent's forgiveness yesterday on a walk we took to honor the end of our marriage, our divorce made official. And here, believe it or not, I zoom past Kent Avenue near Encinal, with the fog lifting. Crows flap. Ravens. I asked Kent to forgive me for my health food fanaticism, criticisms, controlling behavior, absences, restlessness, for my mysticism, which felt like a betrayal to him. Kent was quiet.

Talking things over, especially after the fact, isn't Kent's way. He didn't ask for forgiveness, nor did he say he forgave me. But as we walked in near rain looping up from Horseshoe Lake onto the Rim Trail where we saw the first tentative spring yellow carpet, somehow forgiveness was all about, in the winter grass and in the first lupine shoots emerging.

I no longer have a father or a husband to shelter me. Both men subscribed to *The Skeptical Inquirer* and had opinions about the world that I was supposed to share—rational and scientific. Free-flung mystical fancy, in their world, was unacceptable. Well, stupid, actually. Flaky. Kent was heard to say, "She went cosmic on me."

That aspect of my nature seemed unacceptable to these men;

dangerous, even. Maybe it's best that our particular marriage "decomposed" or shattered. Maybe we were keeping each other from living fully, being who we really are.

Maybe I'm molting. To heck with my jacket. What the hey. I'm fed up with my old mummy mode, afraid of unraveling transformation. I guess I can't avoid the unknown darkness of metamorphosis. The changes seem terrifying, but there's no going back. Enough caterpillar clinging to my many stumbling feet, clutching a tattered way-of-being jacket around me, blinding hood around nodding head.

Besides, Mom has a row of warm coats in her bottomless basement. Even Nanny's mink stole wrestles for space on a crowded rack.

Maybe it's best we can't see what's coming in our lives or we'd be immobilized. We'd never marry, we'd never divorce, we'd never have children, we'd never be born. And God knows we'd never die. Yet maybe death of all kinds is the most freeing and creative experience possible. Paradoxically, yes, the most enlivening. Maybe every primal loss calls forth a rush of creativity and life.

The fog's luminous in sunrise. Farmworkers dig in rows in G-d's mini-storage, which surely has room for the whole town of Live Oak where I whiz past, honest, Ash street, fields aglow. Rows of aspen arms reach up like electrified upside-down squirrels' tails.

I realize that inviting friends to gather last night to help with my "passages" was a way of flagging down my soul: come forth! Bring candles, women, spheres, wine. Bring ten of everything, by chance, even ten tulips with yellow center stars. Bring solace. And my soul—whatever that may be—answered within and without: here I am with you, Sue, bringing chocolate, summoning friends in a circle, each a point of light with party favors.

The mystical rabbis (including Jesus) teach that one has to be alone to contemplate and honor and enter *Ein Sof,* the infinite. Alone like the hawk, the field of mustard, each tree, this oak, never touching another. Like each apple left on these trees alone and dangling. Alone and falling. Alone and shattered.

When shattered, I'm told, we can begin to mend, *tikkun,* Hebrew for "repair." We can experience rebirth, begin to take in the infinite, through cracks that let in the light. Even me, this solitary woman? I wonder. One woman and all souls, this morning, driving through lifting fog, gathered in God's mini-storage.

> Teach me, like you, to drink creation whole
> And casting out my self, become a soul.
> —RICHARD WILBUR

IS THERE ANYTHING in your life that needs to fall apart? What are you holding together because of fear or lack of time? What outer shelter might you have to release to fully allow the creative force within and without to shelter you in the core way you need?

Find a way to honor who you are and who you are becoming. Create a spontaneous gathering for yourself when you're experiencing loss. One or two friends or family members will do. Any number. Dream what you need into being. Find poems you like, songs, music. Turn a table, a room, or your whole house into a cathedral for a ceremony for yourself. Gather in a circle as humans have since prehistoric times. Include earth, air, fire, and water—holy water that you've gathered from a wild place. Kazoos. Balloons. Chocolate. Wine. Whatever you love. Do this often for yourself and each other, fashioning your own deep and wide shelter.

> But if you hide All-under-heaven with
> All-under-heaven there's nothing to get lost.
> This is the great fact that dawns
> from the heart of things.
> —CHUANG TZU

24

poppa's ashes

.

Silent friend of many distances,
feel how your breath enlarges all of space.
Let your presence ring out like a bell into the
   night. . . .
Move through transformation, out and in.
                                   —RAINER MARIA RILKE

Small Midwestern towns drift
like orderly constellations of golden lights in scattering grids on
the prairie, small galaxies, the Pleiades twinkling, as my plane
curves toward Chicago and winter snow. The pilot, in his warm
wool coat, no doubt, warns of freezing fog and drizzle in Chicago.
From the larger place, here, above, the storm we're entering looks
luminous, cocoon-like. I dive with the plane into white unknown.
Amber lights appear everywhere in the sky, on the ground, with
houses and trees. We land, surrounded by snow like white ash.

In the morning my brothers and I sit around the kitchen table in Chicago with Mom, retelling the day Poppa died nearly a year ago. Mom says her parents knew exactly what to do when someone died. First, call Mr. Furth, friendly funeral director, and he'd tell you which coffin to use. Following custom at such times can be comforting. The Talmud is filled with rules and proscriptions for what to do in every situation, how to be in the world. Or else. Cremation is taboo.

In wide-open territory outside custom and tradition in honor of atheist Poppa, I discover I'm more custom-bound than I like to think. And at first I'm uncomfortable that we have no ritual form to follow.

"Heeere's Julian," John announces like a TV emcee, as Rich appears holding a white-and-blue shopping bag emblazoned with a fluttering dove. We're all goofy in the presence of Poppa's ashes, which I secretly believe I've already dispersed invisibly in Wisconsin's Lake Sissabagama with Poppa in my imagination.

Rich opens the cardboard box as if it contains a mini-pizza. He reaches in and grasps the see-through bag, caressing ashes, poking them through plastic with his fingers like a kid with a wad of clay. Oldest son, somehow entitled, touching the untouchable, Richard puts us at ease. "What there is," he says, "is ashes with some pieces of bone."

"There's a blue pail under the sink," John suggests, as we discuss logistics. No! I fiercely veto the pail and search for a round, melon-size covered pot I made years ago on the potter's wheel, when centering perfectly became a mission. The fragile sphere with a curved lid, glazed matte brown with "Sue's Soup," became a gift to my parents. I had no idea it would become an urn to hold my father's ashes. I'm insistent. This is where the ashes belong.

Holding the globe in my hands here in the kitchen, I feel less wobbly, as if the pot I centered is now centering me like the piece of clay I shaped with my hands years ago.

"We'll take big spoons along," Mom suggests. "I'm going to use my fingers," Rich says. He recently helped scatter his father-in-law Bud's ashes and speaks with worldly experience. "Oh Pa, what are we doing to you!" Mom laments, remembering that Poppa said, "Just don't embarrass me" when she asked what he wanted after he died.

Mom comes forth with an ice cream scoop and sends John for a silver spoon. "No, the bigger one," she instructs.

White snow drifts everywhere. It's below zero in the wind. We walk to the garage past icy clumps of clematis with pinwheel seeds. Rich wears Julian's blue denim jacket, too thin, I think. Rich is literally allergic to cold. We're off to the Indiana Dunes house Mom and Dad sold before he died. In her quilted coat and purple fleece hat, Mom looks like a kid bunched in a snowsuit to make angels in the snow. The boxed ashes shift between us in the back seat and the empty brown bowl nests in the blue pail between my feet.

John drives down Cornell in bright sunshine, ten A.M., through Jackson Park, past the Field House with foot-long icicles hanging from eaves, past Stoney Island Supermart. We soar onto the Chicago Skyway above pristine snow on rooftops.

We plan our route. "Grandpa, we're gonna scatter you all over the world," Mom proclaims as blackbirds flurry above white roofs in South Chicago with smokestacks on factories that seem prehistoric. "Those look obsolete," I say. Mom agrees: "This bridge is falling apart. It needs painting. The whole country's going out."

Bundled in eight layers, I take notes, scrawling fast in my journal trying to catch what everyone says, even me, as we create a haphazard farewell for my father.

For months I've been singing the gloomy oldie "One is the loneliest number, one is the loneliest number," trying to free myself. Thinking about Kabbalah, Jewish mystical oneness, I change my chant to "One is the holiest number, one is the holiest number." These words swirl inside my head when Mom holds up her hands like a kid with fingers crossed and whispers, "My fingers are like this. I don't know why, Sue. So far everything's been going so much better than I'd hoped."

The road to Dune Acres on Lake Michigan crunches under snow. "There's no more train station here, no more flag stop," Mom says. "That's a real loss." A loss? Her husband's ashes are tucked under her elbow. We pass cattails fluffing into seed.

"There used to be an ice rink here," John comments. Mom laments, "It's gone. Nothing's as good as it used to be." We turn left on Fern Lane and unexpectedly the mailbox still reads "JR Goldsmith," like a marker. In memoriam. As if we're driving into the past.

Rich and I transfer ashes to my brown bowl. The present can change the past, I realize, remembering the wheel, spattered with clay, centering my bowl. I'm grateful it's round like one of the ten spheres of the Kabbalah's tree of life mapping the nature of the universe. Waiting to be shattered.

As Mom digs in snow alongside the house with her long silver spoon, her best, her impulse seems animal-like. She scoops through drifts to bury the first ashes in a little grave where one of Poppa's woodpiles used to be. *Ribbono shel olam*, I say quietly, Hebrew for "master of the universe." These aren't the right words.

Rich digs into the bowl with his hands and sails ashes over the snow, shouting, "Good-bye, Pop!" These are the right words.

Heartened, I reach into my bowl and dash ashes where some of Poppa's hundreds of daffodils are hidden, planted for me, dormant, and get grit in my eye. John walks backward out of the driveway, casting ashes, silent. Mom says, "We're giving Julian lots of resting places."

"Oh my God, Mom, your car's filling with Poppa dust," I say, thoughtless. We drive down the short road from the dunes house to Lake Michigan. "I don't want him in the lake," Mom says. "I want him on the sand."

Ignoring Mom as if we were little kids, John and I dash across the wildly frozen beach, a gnarled landscape of icy, clumped snow, dazzling in late morning sun. It's frigid in the wind, well below zero. Clutching the brown bowl, I spin as I cast with my hands, getting Poppa's ashes into my eyes and hair and in a fine silt over my black pants. John takes the bowl as we lumber toward the lake roiling into caves and tunnels of thick ice with crashing waves. We fling ashes toward the water as the wind blows them back at us. John wields the silver spoon, dipping ashes into blowholes blasting water through ice. Here's where I feel the wildest spirit of my father. I hurl ashes into the edge of waves, shouting, "I love you, Poppa."

Mom and Rich wait at the entrance to the beach, slightly sheltered from the wind. Back in the car, Mom murmurs, "I'm just sorry Gramps isn't along." Simultaneously Rich and John say, "He is."

Half of Poppa's ashes remain in the bowl tucked in the bucket between my feet. We'll cast them near the university. I wonder what the bowl will hold next. Maybe I'll make myself small and slip inside one day when I'm ready to die, curl in the centering darkness.

We're all strangely exhilarated. Mom exclaims, "I couldn't have hoped for a better day. Just a few degrees warmer." We guess it's about five degrees outside. "I like this cold," I insist. "That makes it a sacrifice," Mom muses, missing the point, as I sing in my head, revising, "One is the holiest number, one is the holiest number," ash making my skin gray, under my nails, all over my journal, making pages scratchy, messing with the ink. Here. These gritty pages in my journal, a lake of words, resting place for a trace of Poppa's ashes. These letters formed with ink and Poppa's powdery bones.

25

godseye

The eye sees only what the mind is prepared
to comprehend.
—Henri Bergson

In Greece one spring, my British
friend Suna pointed out "the eye of God" in a church perched on a
huge outcropping in Petra (Greek for "rock"), a town on the island of Lesvos. Spooked, we stared into an ominous eye on the
ceiling painted in a bathtub-size inset oval. I hadn't even thought
to look up. I wonder how many magical things I simply don't see.
The wide-open eye spied on us as if a disapproving giant crouched
outside, peering through an egg-shaped hole.

Pilgrims on their knees, our guidebook informed us, clamber
up 114 carved rock steps to pray under the eye of God where Suna
and I wandered uneasily with her tall, gentle son, Heron, and her
tempestuous son, Storm. Maybe, perched on this huge rock altar
under the eye of God after a long pilgrimage, seekers find answers

to their prayers. Maybe the journey itself becomes the answer, shifting their vision.

Last week, while making boxes by the creek with me, Dan said, "You make your boxes like altars. I tend to treat mine like paintings and give things time to decide where they want to go themselves." As I place things together, bits of litter shift to look like a mischievous eye that stares up at me as if someone's spying from underground, no matter that it's really a blue thumbtack in a silver pop-top tab. Making collage boxes, like shooting photos, loosens up the way I see.

Dan's right. I'm arranging the box like a funky little shrine. I glue cut-out words from a water label "at the source" on a red background near yellow peeled from a tequila bottle with stripes like cartoon sunrays.

"I like this box," he says, "because it's funny and it looks like an eye." Then he says, laughing, "I think everything looks like an eye." I ask, "How about a tree?" He ponders, "Well, a tree doesn't look much like an eye." Just then we laugh as a small beetle crawls across the table, iridescent, black globe shiny, like a living, walking eye.

That day taught me a different way of working and looking at things. I got a glimpse into another person's way of seeing.

Some collage boxes themselves help me see. I know I can perceive things playfully, openly, or with gloominess, even blinders. Seeing itself is a creative act, I realize.

In the boxes, colors and shapes become landscapes alive in small tableaux. Glass becomes water. A square of dry orange peel becomes a window reflecting sun. The pop-top is a frame, a silver portal with sky peeking through. The godseye reminds me to see loosely, broadly, playfully, colorfully, and to gather or paint or write or even enter what I see.

> In the time of darkness we have never
> been closer to the light.
> —MEISTER ECKHART

GATHER OBJECTS TO MAKE AN ALTAR or a shrine for a small box or for a table top or mantel or windowsill in your home. Look around. What catches your eye? What do you see? Is there a stone that wants to go into your pocket? A twig or coin or shell or leaf? What do they look like? What do they help you see? Even in the house, you might find small objects to move or glue into a shrine, or place on a surface to admire. What do they suggest to you when they're together? What do they help you understand? Where is there a hint of beauty you might never have noticed before? What prevented you from seeing it? What meaning does it bring to your life?

Make one box like an altar. Make another splashing color like a painting.

> Every man takes the limits of his own vision
> for the limits of the world.
> —ARTHUR SCHOPENHAUER

26

angels in encinal:
a pretty how town

.

If the doors of perception were cleansed,
everything would appear as it is, infinite.
—WILLIAM BLAKE

Ragtag packs of wild kids, cir-
cling and faceless, rush into the "multipurpose" cafeteria at Encinal School. What the heck am I doing with two or three classes of
fourth and fifth graders along with frazzled teachers in what looks
like a swirl of chaos? It's social time after lunch and the wired kids
chatter like a flock of cedar waxwings full of fermenting pyracan-
tha berries. I ask for words and toss phrases on the dusty board,
but I can't even begin to catch their attention. Almost ready to call
it quits before we begin, I idly reach for my stash of words taped
on tickets.

I scoop handfuls of words from their blue velvet bag, and we adults dole them out with a sense of hopelessness. We're in over our heads. To our great surprise, the packs of kids quiet down almost immediately as they begin to play with words taped on tickets. Admit one. It seems like a small miracle when I notice the delicate features and twinkling eyes of beautiful children who moments earlier seemed to be rapscallions. I might forget the transforming magic of words, but the kids remind me.

When we begin a group poem that I thought would be playful, hands begin waving and I drop my agenda as hushed kids tell me how to arrange their words on the board,

> Yesterday breathes
> words burn
> soft craters
> in my soul.
> Visionary pain
> enters the sky.

The elusive poem alchemy settles in. Every child wants to tell me his or her words. The kids crave a chance to play with language. Some hoard words in piles, others spread them like a fan. Small groups of girls arrange them in rows and pore over them like treasure. These are simply words: *fiddle, Brazil, Bengal tiger.*

Sikh children with hair in turbans begin to look like slender saints to me when they're calm and focused. Like angels. *Angel,* a word I normally resist (like *unicorn* and *rainbow*), becomes the theme running through our poems after the phrase *waking angels* from a word ticket lands on the blackboard first.

Michael is stuck, although he lines up dozens of words—*hurricane, neverending, colorful, dance, surround, ghost.* I encourage Michael to begin to write with that good old staple phrase: I am. "I am a neverending colorful dance surrounding a ghost," we compose. On his own, Michael writes, "My soul is blinded by a bat/ searching in a boiling available code/ going through rich leaves/ raining black and white." He begins to write nonstop, entranced.

"I want just one more word," another child tells me, reaching into the blue velvet bag. "Murmurs," we say together quietly. His brown eyes shift to musing and he walks off to add *murmurs* to his paper. "How do you spell *star*? How do you spell *endless*? How do you spell *candle*?" the kids ask me. "What does *maelstrom* mean?" A hurricane, a whirlpool. I watch a young girl's eyes take on a faraway look as she wanders to her seat with *maelstrom* in her hand. "What does *treacherous* mean? *Stereo abandoned*?" On one boy's paper, *ground* is moved and a word is added in front of it, *unveiling ground.* A small girl comes to me with a secret. She holds up her ticket and whispers with delight, "I've got *wildest light*."

"I'm a scolded prank," writes one rangy boy, and then he adds, "The wind is a distant lullaby." In addition to "I am," the kids are choosing from a list of starters such as "I wish, I remember, I forget, I want to be, I will be . . ." I glance at Thor's paper and see "the silver instinct of the glowing ornament." I read the phrase "I want to be the glow of dreaming eyes, a ruby flower."

I see

I forget my business suit.
I want to be saltwater.

Ten-year-old Melissa fills her page with dreamsense, beginning

> I am like a bamboo dandelion clock,
> the one you cannot hear. . . .

Kurtis writes that it is

> Hard to forget a horsewinged grandpa.
> Nonsensed grandpa peeks among us.

After class I read stacks of poems scrawled in dull pencil in large child letters, riddled with misspellings. I copy into my journal a poem by nine-year-old Sarah, ending

> Black and white magic is in the air all around us
> while different
> inventions
> are being made
> in the heads of sleeping children . . .
> we are all full of gentleness
> and shyness as well.
> The kayak will break
> when the moon grazes behind the mountains
> and the butterflies fly no more.

I'm not sure where poems come from. They often seem like mysterious visitors bringing unexpected treasure. We conjure them out of ourselves. It's as if each poem is a container for the soul's voice, fashioned from words we shape into a form that offers a glimpse of the soul itself, the soul made visible.

After the session one little girl stays at her table immersed in a book of poems by e. e. cummings. She's soaking up the freedom of his words here in Encinal, full of waking angels along with cummings's "anyone," who "lives in a pretty how town," like this young girl, "with up so floating many bells down."

WORDS HAVE AN UNEXPECTED, often transformational effect, even on large groups of children. Individual words might seem trivial, abstract, ordinary, but time and again I see words in random patterns shift people into another realm. Words are possibilities, they can act as visitors from a place we've never explored and they can be gathered in ways that help us express a vision of who we are—an expanded, exhilarating, and limitless sense of ourselves.

None of this makes headlines. *Angels Writing in Encinal*. But the phenomenon can happen anywhere. In your kitchen. On a bus. Open a book of poems. Gather or steal some words. Cut words out of magazines, or out of a journal of poems. Tape them onto colored paper or tickets. Let them help you conjure a larger way of being and begin a conversation with your soul, a glimpse of wildest light.

So then, the poet really is the thief of fire.
—ARTHUR RIMBAUD

27

---

first words

·

The words came without their numbers.
At first they came in pairs
like animals onto the ark.

    Tangerine came with hustle
    splendor with taboo.

Some made a little electrical *ping*
when they touched the ground.

They hadn't been uttered
and were all still shiny and intact.
Nothing had been broken by them yet.

Birds draped words over their bodies
like stars of Bethlehem,
    saffron celestial surge surrender

Their colors were so bright no one,
had anyone been present,
could have looked at them directly.
As if they'd just come from the sun.

I would be ignorant as the dawn.

Words like this kept falling from somewhere.

Not like rain, though it was raining,
   kangaroo flame
   phosphorescent spin
words came and wouldn't stop coming,
   imbue terrestrial seed soon

in a rush
in wildest light
that first
wet morning.

          —S. W.

28

dragonfly haiku

·

To-day I saw the Dragon Fly
Come from the wells where he did lie;
An inner impulse rent the veil
Of his old husk; from head to tail
Came out clear plates of sapphire mail.
He dried his wings—like gauze they grew:
Thro' crofts and pastures wet with dew
A living flash of light he flew.

—ALFRED, LORD TENNYSON

 Mini–living biplanes hover over
the road and whir over my windshield in an updraft as I drive
home along the Sacramento River. Dragonflies swarm in pockets
like gnats with translucent wings reminding me of Wonder
Woman's magic glass airplane in childhood comic books. Wonder
Woman crouched in warrior stance on her plane's see-through

wing, flying to daring rescues. Here dragonflies whiz over farm workers bending to scatter seeds of beans and squash.

As I drive, I jot down ragged little haikus, noticing that dragonflies almost seem to be made of haiku—with wings lines one and three, bodies center line. Five, seven, five. Wings, body, wings. Living haiku, rare and yet common, airy and substantial at the same time.

> Dragonflies whir low
> like the heartbeat of haiku
> skimming Lonestar Road.

Dragonflies take off. There's something ancient and mythical as well as ordinary about them, just like haiku. Dragonflies might whiz by any road in any field and yet, they're jewel-like. Fleeting. Part dragon, part myth, and, like fireflies and poems, magical.

Japanese poet Issa wrote more than one thousand haikus about bugs, Robert Hass tells us in *The Essential Haiku*. "Don't worry spiders/ I keep house/ casually." Issa loved the comical and ordinary, Hass writes: "Climb Mount Fuji snail/ but slowly, slowly." Every Japanese haiku has a keynote seasonal phrase, Hass says. "Spring rain" defines early spring, and "rain of spring," late. Haiku celebrates both what's timeless and what's transitory and cyclical. "This is a world of dew" is a Buddhist mantra, Hass writes. A world of dragonflies.

I've been reading Clark Strand's *Seeds from a Birch Tree* about making haiku a daily, meditative practice. As I scribble lines I'm an eager beginner following an ancient tradition.

f o o l s g o l d

·

Nuzzling the grass
a black mare wanders slowly
earth becomes her drum.

Can you catch morning
quicksilver dragonfly
darting here near me?

Turning onto Lonestar Road, I notice a curled dragonfly husk in my windshield wiper, crisp and dry like an old leaf. I lift it out and prop it above my steering wheel, where its folded body seems inflated like a yellow and black mini-snakeskin windsock in a slight breeze. Window wings, partitioned with black string veins, are still perky and alert. But the haiku spirit has left the dragonfly, along with life and flight.

I find another dragonfly in the wipers, still alive and soft. A line like Morse code—dash, dot, dash—carries secrets in yellow and black where the wing curves. The body's segmented like a snake. Giant eyes fill the head like pearly gray eggs. I stop the car outside Colusa and set the dying dragonfly in the shade under a walnut tree, his head wobbling like a marionette, eyes wide, purplish, marbled with waves of lenses, delicate and bold. I sing a song to it that I wrote just before my grandmother Rosel died. I'm imagining how the world might look through oceanic eyes filling my head.

A week later, passing fields of sunflowers with their heads akimbo, guarded by silvery streamers, I'm wondering what the opposite of dragonfly might be, although all I see are butterflies.

The answer rattles on the road in front of me, a cement mixer. Then I notice the tank has a long white insect face and a snout, also wobbling like the head of a marionette. The snout funnels cement to make concrete slabs. Aha, there's the opposite of dragonfly.

> No spring dragonflies
> just slow summer butterflies
> float into my day.

IMAGINE SLIPPING into a bug consciousness. Jot a few haiku— five-seven-five syllables—from inside the bug. Play with haiku in your journal for a while. Notice the season, the day, what's happening around you right now that might be part of natural cycles. Focus on insects, birds, sky, leaves, blossoms. If it's winter and you're inside, what's in your kitchen that's temporary, like Rocky Road ice cream, or what's just outside the window?

29

mirror kiss:
vernous

.

> I know nothing in the world that has as much
> power as a word. Sometimes I write one,
> and I look at it, until it begins to shine.
> —EMILY DICKINSON

Words that are both nouns and verbs can add punch to our poems and all our writing. They encompass both stuff *(bicycle)* and movement *(bicycle)*. I like to call these noun-verb words *vernous*. They follow an article *(the* or *a)* or the infinitive *to.* The flood; to flood. The finger; to finger. A swallow; to swallow. A whiz; to whiz. Many one-syllable verbs are nouns as well: *Lurch. Spin. Sting. Head.* I've been gathering vernous for years, just as I gather *litter* and *stuff* for my *boxes.*

Nouns define "things" in our world. *Bandage* (noun-verb). When we name something—matchstick, for example—we can see it more clearly. Nouns have to do with naming, defining boundaries that help us both see and be in a relationship with what we name.

Verbs are action, filled with life, because life is movement. *Bandage*. Gardens are full of vernous: *plant, green, sprinkle, hose, bud, sprout, flower, bloom, stem, leaf, blossom, bug, nibble, seed, shade, branch, spread, stalk*. The word *garden* itself is a noun-verb.

Words that are both nouns and verbs seem especially alive, powerful, and connected to us. *Question. Sink. Plug. Sock. Foil. Sizzle. Spiral. Tease. Lure. Spell. Sparkle.* Vernous give our expression force and substance. Almost alive themselves, vernous infuse our talk and writing with life. Vernous move with *muscle* and *sound*. They *pack* a *wallop*. They have a particular poem-like compression and punch. *Storm. Thunder. Rain. (Spring horse fling surprise leap latch splash flash swing shift flounder.)*

Many abstractions are both nouns and verbs.

Love and its opposites, *fear* and *hate,* are vernous. *Lie* is a vernou, but *truth* is not. *War* is a vernou, but *peace* is not. Playing with words in a workshop once, we decided that *war,* a monster vernou abstraction, may well have as an opposite the innocent word *dimple*—a vernou that implies childlike beauty and life.

For a while I was obsessed with vernous. I made lists pages long, alphabetized and in categories. I warn you now! Vernous, noun-verbs—call them vouns or nerbs if you prefer—are strong, versatile, and addictive. *Take care!* (Both vernous.)

In *The Way of Zen,* Alan Watts wrote, "In English the differences between things and actions are clearly, if not always logically, distinguished, but a great number of Chinese words do duty for both nouns and verbs—so that one who thinks in Chinese has little difficulty in seeing that objects are also events, that our world is a collection of processes rather than entities."

Yes! Our world is made of "processes rather than entities." Everything's in motion. *Fall. Spring. Intrigue.* "Objects are also events." *Hail* is a *round* bit of *ice* and it's also a *storm.* A *stream* is alive, dazzling, and capable of *flood*ing. I think there may well be many more vernous in English than Watts noticed, including *water* and *sun, sources* of all life.

BEGIN TO GATHER VERNOUS for fun. Here are some for a start: *cloud plug dust toast tilt fish serenade cow broke ladle throttle cream slug steam stop play signal grin fragment collapse number marble creep drip stretch disguise tattoo tantrum chicken shrink court smile glow play spell wind tear star shade moon lisp squall joke drop.*

Look for the vernous below (i.e., *sentence*).

Write a sentence using several vernous, for example,

When I water, the wet ground has a laugh. Or, finger the echo slant.

Choose two vernous for a title, such as "Mirror Kiss." Create a small scene or scenario that is centered on vernous. This can be a paragraph, a letter, or a poem. You might want to choose categories of vernous, such as garden words. Create a meadow of vernous and play there.

You might choose words of the body: *elbow, shoulder, finger, knee.*

Or sports: *bat, swing, toss, shoot, kick, swim.*

Or dance: *tango, waltz, swing, spin, twirl, pirouette, cha-cha, stroll, jitterbug, samba.*

See where the vernous want you to go. Dream hollow. No-tice if your writing with vernous has extra punch. Try a haiku with vernous:

> Fall into winter
> a forecast of snow showers
> frosts our glimpse of moon.

Revise a short piece of writing or poem. Pepper it with vernous and see what you think. I've shifted the first two sections of my poem "Pirate's Words" to "Pirate's Bluff," filled with vernous for fun.

PIRATE'S BLUFF

Scratch tease sting ribbons,
I cast words aside
with a wave of my hand
a twist of wrist (though
your love notes fill me).

I scan the house of light
after lunch with your mother
at the fountain of sighs
and wish only
to fathom
you.

30

clock's breath

·

You came into this world as a radiant package of cosmic wonders, as an unspeakably sublime bolt of primordial resonance, as a barely coalesced jumble of blinding beauty—and all your parents wanted was a good little girl or good little boy.

—ROBERT BLY

(as paraphrased by columnist Rob Brezsny)

To observe without evaluating is the highest form of intelligence.

—JIDDU KRISHNAMURTI

Determined not to listen, Patrick flops his head on top of his desk among a restless gathering of kids, ages eleven to seventeen, labeled SED—severely emotionally disabled—by conventional wisdom. I ask the kids for their name and a word. No one responds. Saying a word might be dangerous.

·

I remember feeling scared in a gathering of writers when someone asked us each for one word. I couldn't decide between *cougar* and *toe*. Why couldn't I think of a better word? How could I be so dumb? Putting out even one word can be scary. One word can be judged not good enough. At workshops now I pass out books of poems for gathering words. Spelling is no issue and we see how writers use words. Besides, it's fun to steal words from famous poets. *Riverhills. Snowy. Evening. Tantalize.*

After I hand out word tickets, a few words are spoken and I chalk them on the board. Franklin, an expressionless, rotund African American boy, gives me his name. I ask him if I can put *Franklin* on the board and where he'd like it. He pauses and then risks, "Before *midnight*," a word placed earlier next to *boulders.* I read out loud, *Franklin's midnight boulders.* Franklin laughs at this zaniness, king of boulders, opening to a larger idea of who he might be. Giant of the night. Everyone begins to perk up and listen.

What's the opposite of *midnight*? I ask, insisting there's no right answer and no way to make a mistake. Words begin to fly out: *dawn, noon, numbers, dust, clouds, air, dreams.* Spinning out these words, especially opposites, allows us to expand our concept of the universe and who we are within it. The kids come alive at their desks.

Someone says *I don't know* when I ask for a word. I love putting *I don't know* on the board. Socrates said, "All I know is that I know nothing," I explain. If we don't know anything, hooray! We can begin to expand. It's all these categories of "knowing" that can get us in trouble.

Someone's word ticket says *the curves of woman,* and we place it after *I don't know.* The line reads, *I don't know the curves of woman.* Franklin, now a star, says there's a word missing after *woman.* The word *yet.* His timing is perfect. I read, *I don't know the curves of woman, yet.* We have a good laugh and now the group is safe and rolling.

Words fill the board. *Clock* crouches in the corner next to *breath,* for *clock's breath.* I ask what *clock's breath* might be. Patrick, without hesitating, says *time.* He's increasingly animated, finding a place, playing with words, to engage his boundless creativity.

Chaos lands on the board. All kids love the word *chaos.* We talk about making up words and Patrick uses *chaos* and *anarchy* to coin *anarchaotic,* and then he adds *lawfulize.* Later I learn that Patrick likes to make bombs.

The kids are bouncing up and down wanting more words on the board—*tangent, surge, cottage*—and time is running out. Clock's breath. I ask them to write down their words. They use phrases like *mellow mechanical* and *correct puzzles* and *low moons* that day as we commune in the wordpool and the safe realm of poems that rises up in and around us among the words—a realm where no one's emotionally disabled, severely or no.

> I didn't want to say good-bye to that day.
> —WILLIAM, "SED" fifth grader in our class

WHERE AND HOW HAVE YOU BEEN LABELED by yourself or others? I feel uncomfortable if I'm introduced as a "poet." I haven't been writing poems. I don't want to be called anything. Have you been called gifted? Impatient, a control freak, a dilettante, a saint, an artist, a delinquent, an angel? A good girl. A bad boy. Finicky?

Sensitive? How do these judging labels limit you and curb your creative freedom, even if they might sound positive?

Play with labeling and unlabeling yourself. Wild thing, prude, king of hearts, unruly queen, leopard woman, jaguar man, snail creature, whatever it takes to shift out of labels and limitations, "good or bad." Turn even those concepts upside down and be a bankrobber, beggar, someone about to be put to death. Someone with Alzheimer's, who may well be seeing everything anew all the time. See how your body reacts to these labels.

Write down the opposite of what you've heard or told yourself are the worst and the best things about you. Bold, timid, shy, adventurous, devil-may-care. Freely expressive. Jot them down. See if words can help you shift.

Write down labels others have used to describe you. Choose one that makes you uncomfortable, and do something (or write about it!) that would "undo" that label.

Play with your identity. Let words help you experience the playful sense that you're none of these things, you're much larger, boundless. Rather than limiting definitions, we need a more expansive idea of who we are. Feel the freedom of simply being alive. Allow the mystery of yourself to go unnamed.

> As long as I am this or that, I am not all things.
> —MEISTER ECKHART

> Your only limitations are those you set up in your mind,
> or permit others to set up for you.
> —OG MANDINO

31

....

diamond dust

.

Perhaps you can write better if you leave
the mistakes.
—Jorge Luis Borges

On the two-hour leg of my flight
from Cleveland to Sacramento, soaring from Cincinnati to Salt
Lake City, I decide to avoid conversation. I plan to nap, read about
Fellini, and glance at Tom Cruise in *Jerry Maguire* on the airplane
screen with no sound. I enjoy watching silent movies in airplanes,
imagining dialogue, playing deaf.

It's amazing how much can come to pass in two tucked-away
hours, flying over a stretch of earth on a spring morning. Time
can expand and become huge or shrink and disappear.

Ignoring Tom Cruise I jot an excerpt from *Falling Boy*, by
David Long, into my journal: "He and Olivia lie adjacent in the
semi-dark, and the last thing she says is, 'See you on the other

shore.' " I want to remember these words. "See you on the other shore." I want to say them to someone I love at night.

Over the Midwest I peer out the window and notice the man beside me glance out, too. "Not much of a view," I say, "just a wing," never imagining where my witless remark will lead. The man—a weary version of a younger Paul Newman, trim with gray hair and blue eyes—says, "Well, it's a beautiful wing, lovely abstract diagonal across the sky."

Setting down my magazine, I scribble in my journal, "Are most people writers? Maybe. Some of us just put it on paper." Then I note what I'm reading, that Pramoedya Ananta Toer, imprisoned in Indonesia, was allowed no paper. Other inmates memorized his tales. Seventeen novels came from Toer in prison.

A rush of blonde hair thick as a horse tail hangs beside the seat in front of me, bright in sunlight from the window. Individual hairs curl like tendrils on a plant seeking sun.

My neighbor and I silently eat dry airline sandwiches over plastic packets. Then he asks if I'm a professor, because of my books and notes. A professor! I say, "No, I write," and show him *poemcrazy*. He's a professor of law, he tells me. Flipping through the pages of *poemcrazy,* he quotes Merwin: "Everything has to do with listening."

To feel comfortable in a place, he says, he needs to listen to its history, the stories and tales. His son (not the one killed rock climbing, I learn) likes to know the chemical basis of things. This man sees me as grounding myself with words. *Haphazard,* we agree, is a good one. For now I'll call him Paul.

His description of the wing, I say, sounded like the words of a writer. I confess that I wrote it down. We talk about writers like Toer who don't actually put words on paper. Paul says he's reading the *Iliad,* and reminds me that Homer was illiterate and blind in a time there was no Braille. He'd fill in lines with stock epithets, like "wine dark sea." Homer probably recited his rhythmic poems, repeated and improved them, and listeners took them down. In Indonesia, Paul remarks, it may not be much different.

In my own writing, I tell Paul, I resist bringing chapters or poems into final form because I love to tinker and rearrange. I'm usually more interested in the process than in the product. Increasingly when I make collage boxes I don't like to use glue. I gather stuff into matchboxes with sliding tops and let the contents shift like a kaleidoscope, almost alive.

When I tell Paul he has a way with words, he argues that for someone who stuttered and was dyslexic, it's hard for him to believe. He never felt intelligent. In speech therapy he was taught to put letters on scooters and bicycles, to "get them going in the right direction." Being bright isn't important to him, he insists. Every child is like a seed and nobody, especially the parent, he stresses, knows what the seed will grow into. Every child can grow into something wonderful, he says with sadness. I imagine he's thinking about his dead son.

Kids labeled dyslexic often seem gifted to me, I offer, like my student Terra, a fourth grader who dictated her poems. Paul doesn't like the term *gifted.* He thinks any label is damaging. I realize he's right about the danger of labels. The power of words.

Dyslexic. Gifted and *talented. Severely emotionally disabled. Illiterate. Crazy.* I tell Paul I often see what could be labeled as failings or trials turn into blessings. My nervous breakdown, for one.

We glance up at *Jerry Maguire,* which Paul says he's already seen. The heart of the movie, he said, is Maguire's learning how to love his wife. Twice divorced, Paul says love is one of those seed things. You can't force it.

Paul claims he learns by "going where he has to go." He can't remember the name of the poet who wrote this but promises to send me the poem. We talk about ways of seeing the universe, about the three wise men who studied the stars and the theory that stars don't move. The wise men, Paul explains, saw the stars as representing the unmoving mover, God. Around the year zero, sages began to believe that the fixed sphere of stars moved. Paul pours out information as I scrawl in my journal. He's a law professor, I remember, used to lecturing for students taking notes.

When I tell Paul how I remet Jack, my English teacher when I was fourteen, he remarks, "Souls recognize each other. The passage of time is unimportant." We're coming in over the Great Salt Lake, vast, icy, barren and parched yet wet, a sprawling crystalline basin in a ring of snowy mountains.

The *Iliad,* Paul comments, is about what it's like to live with death. "Where I am now and in my soul, I feel the death of my son scarred me," Paul muses. "I've lost and lost forever. Who can tell me it will be better? That's why what happened to Achilles is so much more interesting than what happened to the immortal gods," Paul insists. "Human beings are surrounded by death. It's here that people have to face the hardest choices; become heroes."

Paul points out the window past the white tower in a field where he owns part of a new company making equipment to chemically separate things identical by size, such as viruses, bacteria, molecules of plastic, "to help people do things," he explains. "To make miniature electronic circuits, someone may need to polish things with diamond dust. What if this diamond dust is too big?" Paul asks. "In this microscopic world we're picking boulders out of the sandbox in a world ten thousand times smaller than ours."

We land, discussing diamond dust.

Paul promises to send me the poem he loves. He leans over to kiss me on the cheek before we exit, our two hours up. Soon we separate in a line of hurrying travelers. I rush to gate B for my connection to Sacramento, shoulders aching under my stuffed black carry-on. Paul ambles the other way toward the baggage claim, arms swinging free.

A few days later, the familiar poem "The Waking" by Theodore Roethke, one of my favorite poets, arrives in the mail. "It's a remarkably slow poem," Paul observes. I write to thank him and never hear from him again. I imagine him walking off, disappearing in a shifting field of diamond dust that glistens like foolsgold near the Great Salt Lake.

THE WAKING

I wake to sleep, and take my waking slow.
I feel my fate in what I cannot fear.
I learn by going where I have to go.

We think by feeling. What is there to know?
I hear my being dance from ear to ear.
I wake to sleep, and take my waking slow.

Oh those so close beside me, which are you?
God bless the Ground! I shall walk softly there,
And learn by going where I have to go.

Light takes the Tree; but who can tell us how?
The lowly worm climbs up a winding stair;
I wake to sleep, and take my waking slow.

Great nature has another thing to do
To you and me; so take the lively air,
And, lovely, learn by going where to go.

This shaking keeps me steady. I should know.
What falls away is always. And is near.
I wake to sleep, and take my waking slow.
I learn by going where I have to go.

—THEODORE ROETHKE

THINK ABOUT A CHANCE CONVERSATION that deeply affected or changed you. Imagine the challenge of capturing this without paper. Recall a time in your life when life-changing events happened in a very short time. Write about a chance meeting or event that resulted in a life-changing decision. Gather images for a collage that represents this time to you. Give yourself a time limit. Within that time, go slow.

Notice if the process of doing or making something is as important to you as the product that results. Gather for a box and leave the contents free to rearrange themselves. Notice how your ideas and feelings about process and product affect the way you do things in the world.

> "I have a resistance to gluing stones," I say to Mom.
> She laughs. "Yes," she says, "it's sort of sacrilege
> to take a nice wild thing and glue it down."

32

foolsgold and ethel's landing

.

If the fool persists in his folly,
he will become wise.
—WILLIAM BLAKE

My mom always insists that there's not an artistic bone in her body. Somehow she's labeled herself "not creative." She likes to focus on people, not things. Since Poppa's death, she's been withdrawn and a bit numb, less inclined to try new things. She's not sure she wants to be out here with me as we amble into one of Bidwell Park's shady picnic spots in late summer heat by the summer-shallow creek. It's Mom's first visit since I started making daily collage boxes, and it's more than a year since Poppa died. I'm afraid my box-making will bore her, but I resist giving up my current morning practice.

We settle near the creek and Mom begins to scout with me, a surprise. Though Mom looks perky in a bright red shirt and black sneakers, her walking is increasingly hesitant.

When Mom first came to visit me in the co-housing village after Poppa died, I knew she would love my bedroom, with its doors to a balcony looking down the central village path she calls "the avenue," and my den, with its adobe floor and French doors surrounded by lavender. She appreciates these rooms, but the part of the house she truly loves is the landing halfway up the stairs, which offers a pause between two worlds where she can be in a kind of limbo. The landing is neither here nor there. Since Poppa died, Mom's not sure she wants to be alive anymore. A landing is where one takes off and/or comes down from, in flight, with oars or wings, maybe to another world. On the landing, Mom's not really anywhere. She's poised to go either up or down. Her options are open.

If it were her landing, Mom confided, she'd have a window seat or chair there. So as a surprise for her birthday, I created Ethel's Landing. I bought an antique wicker chair (and later found an aluminum pot under the seat that makes us laugh). Now Mom can live on the landing if she wants, with everything she needs in a quiet place between up and down. There are family photos of Poppa; the children and grandchildren; Mom's parents, Rosel and Theodore; and her brother, Elmore. There are flowers, and there are stairs below and stairs above this resting place—like a box the size of a full bed—where you can head up or tumble down, gaze upon the scene below and decide whether or not that's where you want to go.

Today, Mom and I wander about our picnic spot, ready to begin filling a box. I'm pleased she's decided to help me forage, though I assume she'll give it up shortly to read her book. "Look over there," Mom commands. "What's the thing flashing just past that leaf?" Expecting a gum wrapper in trampled picnic dust, I'm delighted to find a small glistening chunk of fool's gold, fingertip size, waiting here for Fool's Goldsmith. Most propitious! "Aha! It's beautiful," I almost yell. "This is a real find, the perfect start for your first box!" It might as well be solid gold, the way the fool's gold shines in my hand, the way it makes me feel, transformed by the alchemy of delight. Emma, enjoying the action, rolls in the dirt, gathering foxtails.

I start to think about the nature of gold—fitting, as my mom's name (and my maiden name) is Goldsmith. Gold is inherently valuable, the most precious metal, "the most malleable and ductile of all the metals," the *American Heritage Dictionary* tells me. And fool's gold is iron or copper pyrite, gold in color, and frequently was mistaken for gold during the various gold rushes. Fool's gold. It's beautiful, but it has no inherent value. The two words are merged into one by play: *foolsgold*.

Finding the foolsgold has Mom hooked. Now she's fully into the spirit of the hunt, rummaging in dusty leaves, eagerly seeking treasure. I'm proud of her for making magic happen for us here. I thought she'd just tolerate my crazy box-making. How I underestimate her!

We glue the golden pyrite in the center and I ask if she wants the box vertical or horizontal. Eyes shut, Mom says she pictures horizontal, although she claims she's thinking vertical. We decide it has to work both ways, true of most paintings and collage, in balance upside down and sideways as well as right side up.

We add a silver spring like a mini-spiral galaxy. The broken green bottle top in a crescent, Mom insists, must go below the silver foil that seems to spill out of it. Of course! I agree. Many of these are Mom's "finds," and we collaborate on decisions. I notice she's walking with stronger strides. All the discernment gained from years of looking at art and collecting paintings and pre-Columbian art with Poppa always in charge, never making the choices herself, seems to take hold now and pour out of her.

Soon Mom has become boss and teacher. I eagerly seek her counsel. The translucent blue plastic straw, Mom assures me, belongs on top, and she directs where to place the bit of blue rubberized wire. Thoughtfully, she decides where to put the eight seeds and the yellow straw as well. Now Mom declares we're finished. We can't add anything else to the box without spoiling it. I would have added more, cluttering up the box the way I frequently do, the way I crowded Ethel's Landing at first, hating to leave anything out.

Now I see that these boxes are like Ethel's Landing, a small realm to enter that's in the world and yet out of this world, a manageable place we can control and rearrange. This box is a haven, a respite where Mom is fully removed from the world "out there" and yet fully engaged in a world of gathering and composing. And it provides a quiet pause between worlds. A small place to go that's neither here nor there.

Today's box with foolsgold seems more valuable than gold, providing a safe, quiet world for Mom where she can experience her creativity and be immersed, leaving behind, for a time, her shaky legs and her temptation to give up.

.

Earth cannot escape heaven, flee it by going up or flee it
by going down; heaven still invades earth,
energizes it, makes it sacred.

—MEISTER ECKHART

WANDER AROUND YOUR HOME and see if there's a spot somewhere
that's especially peaceful or removed, like Ethel's Landing. If you
don't find such a place, you might want to create one. Just a corner
will do, furnished with a cushion—somewhere you can go to
empty your mind and feel like you're neither here nor there.

On your next walk, look for a quiet place that is somehow
out of the world, where you can pause between the realm of your
daily activities and the wild world of nature or action of the city.
You might find this place by water, in the woods, perhaps even in
an alley or on the stairs of an old apartment building. Seek a spot
that feels new to you, that might hold "worthless" surprises, like
fool's gold, or a spiral of silver litter, a place that's small, peaceful,
both in and out of the world. When you're there, settle in. Let
yourself pause. You might want to just be there and do nothing.

3

WORLD AS STUDIO

·

The sun shines not on us but in us. The rivers flow
not past, but through us, thrilling, tingling, vibrating
every fiber and cell of the substance of our bodies,
making them glide and sing.

—JOHN MUIR

33

being a horse

*

You were wild here once. Don't let them tame you.
—ISADORA DUNCAN

When I was a little girl I became a horse. I perfected the whinny and a coltish prance. I galloped, cavorted, grazed, tossed my mane; and, unlike other horses, I read books. *King of the Wind*. That was me. *Black Beauty*. How could humans be so cruel? *Misty of Chincoteague*. I wanted to roam Maine. But it was Walter Farley who took me over the edge into a land of secret passion and longing. *The Island Stallion. The Island Stallion's Fury. The Black Stallion*. I needed to enter that world, be part of the wildness, grandeur, power, danger, and beauty. I needed to ride or be a chestnut stallion with a star on the forehead, an Arabian with no bit or saddle, only extravagant freedom.

It wasn't easy being a horse in school, where I felt suppressed and out of place. At least if I couldn't run wild, I could learn to draw horses: the curve of the neck, the flying front legs stretched out straight and knobby with bunched back legs like a complicated letter *M*. In the margins of notebooks I practiced alert ears, mane and tail in wind, nostrils flaring on a spoon face. Only wild Arabian stallions interested me. I mimicked a classmate who gave me some of her fine sketches.

To me there was nothing more beautiful, sensitive, alive than a horse—than me as a horse. I think being a horse helped me feel a bit detached from the plodding human world, in which I had no power. As a horse I could ignore rules, kick down fences, be anything I wanted outside human ideas. I could neigh loudly and inappropriately. I could buck and rear and trample things. I could race across a field and thunder my creative heart and soul into a swirling force of life with no one watching. A horse could pound or paint with her hooves, write upside-down words in one long sentence like the tail of a storm. A horse could create small tornados in the dust surging up with the force of creation. No one could tell a horse how to do or be anything.

I wanted to spend as much time with other horses as possible. However, I wasn't happy posting for the trot with English-style lessons on a tall, timid chestnut named Stonewall. I longed for the Wild West. As a pre- and early teen I became crazed over cowboys, and I can still sing the theme song of every Western on TV at that time: *The Rebel, Cheyenne, Maverick, Laramie, Sugarfoot, Have Gun Will Travel, Wyatt Earp, Gunsmoke, Rawhide, Bonanza,* all of them. My love shifted back and forth from horses to cowboys, but we were part of each other. Home on the range.

I discovered I belonged in the West when I was three or four and Poppa took us on geology field trips to Laramie, Wyoming, and Leadville, Colorado. Later I would gallop alongside the car in open fields on family trips to the West, leaping buildings and signs. When we drove north from L.A. as a family one summer, I looked longingly at the hazy Sierra Nevada mountains and sensed they were home.

I spent most of two summers at H Bar G Ranch for girls in Estes Park, Colorado. Already scrawny at eleven, I lost seven pounds I was so homesick, but a bay quarter horse named Red-wing was mine the first year and the next year it was Blueberry, a speckly gray known for speed. I brushed, saddled, slipped in the slithery bit, loped, galloped, and, along with all the other girls, fell for the rangy young wrangler named Pete. I lived to hear the words "Lope 'em." I rode in a rodeo. A glossy photo shows wispy me angling Redwing around barrel turns with my tongue curled into the corner of my mouth. "Tumbling Tumbleweeds" became my favorite song.

When Kent and I moved to Turlock, California, I recklessly bought the first horse I looked at, Smoky, because he was part Arab and came to the fence when I called, taking me in with large, gentle eyes. I soon learned he hadn't been gelded early enough to curb stallion behavior. Nevertheless I was determined not to use a bit in his mouth, just a loose hackamore around his nose, and I set out to teach him dressage, a system of horse handling that uses knee signals, delicate touch, and intuitive communication.

One day we were loping in the adjoining field when Smoky decided to cut out for the grazing mares and I couldn't stop him. He galloped toward the fence line and coiled rolls of barbed wire. I jumped off and hit hard, injuring my back. Somehow I got us both back to the pasture. My compression fracture healed in time, but Smoky was more than I could handle. Selling him was heartbreaking. But soon afterward I had two small children, a husband, a house, and a dog. Horses can't live that way.

I missed Smoky at first, but I realized that *having* a horse wasn't as freeing as *being* a horse. Horses don't necessarily want to be "had." *As* a horse, I escaped to a world of spirit and speed where I was free and skittish and sensitive and silent on the steppes or in the Wild West's wide-open spaces.

Our creative nature is like that. Alive, kicking, powerful, and wild, within and without.

WHERE IN YOUR LIFE do you feel boxed or fenced in? Where could you kick down or at least dismantle a fence and expand your boundaries? There are many ways to kick down fences and tap in to what frees you to do what most enlivens you and helps you feel wild. What makes your blood race? Is it time to get on the back of someone's motorcycle? Do you have a wild idea that might transform your business? Is it time to come up with a wild party at work or at home? When's the last time you skied fast? What can you do that brings out your wildness without endangering yourself or other people?

Notice where you feel most compromised by the demanding, taming world of humans. What can you do to open things up for your spirit, your heart, your art? Set aside fifteen minutes today to act like a horse or a bird or a cat. Gallop. Flit. Prowl. Stalk and pounce. Feel the animal energy. Write or paint as an animal, if only in your journal.

You might not want to be a cat, a bird, or a horse—though it's fun to practice your loon call and your howler monkey's roar. You might simply want to buy a feather boa, or dye your hair another color. Go inside to an inner wild garden where you'll find unicorns and other creatures who've always been free. Go there whenever you can, and write memos, do business, draw, sing, make love from that place. The world is waiting for your wildness.

> I should always let my thoughts thunder
> onto the paper in front of me.
> —CHRISTOPHER, sixth grader
> in a workshop at a junior high school
> in Pleasanton, California

34

bopper's songs: rolling with the muse

·

When my daughter was about seven years old
she asked me one day what I did at work.
I told her I worked at the college, teaching
people to draw. She stared back at me,
incredulous, and said, "You mean they forget?"
—HOWARD IKEMOTO

Don't save these songs. Don't worry about
writing them down. We've fallen into a place
where everything is music.

—RUMI

"There was a little girl, once upon a weasel, once upon a weasel . . ." my girl, Elisabeth, nicknamed Bopper (from Elisabop), sang at four. She had wispy white-blonde hair, huge brown eyes, and a dimple on her chin. When she was by herself most everything out of her mouth was a ditty, a mini-Bopper calypso to her own rhythm in a running melodic commentary about what she saw around and inside her. An ongoing song-chronicle bubbled forth as she played, composed for no one in particular. "The air is knocking on the door/ the air has hands/ come in air . . ."

I'd hear bird song in the trees, Bopper song in the yard. Like the birds, singing seemed to be both Bopper's nature and her way of loving the world. She sang, "To love us and to love them, to love every single thing, to love us and to love them, to love everything around." It was hard to catch her song-words because they spilled out fast as if bubbling up from both an inner and outer source, what I call the undersong.

> He can run through
> a chair, a car, a dish
> He can run through a mommy,
> a cloud, plum, cherry . . .
> and when the falling sun comes out . . .
> the fing fing fing fout

Bopper created worlds with berries, petals, leaves, glass animals, and beads and sang about the sparkling world she arranged in her own shifting collages. Sketching on a leaf when she was three, Elisabeth said, "I'd like to draw on the sky." She was immersed in her own form of "art"; though such song-play doesn't neatly fit within the word, which implies intention, design, effort, self-consciousness. Bopper's arrangements and songs emerged before she had any idea there was such a thing as "art," from joy of self-expression, a pure impulse that's in each of us in some form and can be rekindled. (*Impulse:* inner beat or pulse like breath or heartbeat, our connection to the music of the spheres.) "Give air to the heavens," wrote physicist Johannes Kepler, "and there will be music." Catching the impulse of art involves listening within, alone, quiet, safe and free in nature, or surrounded by materials we can make into a personal brew.

Bopper's reverie-composition was unique. Each of us has a distinct "voice" that emerges in our talk, our walk, our paintings, songs, and poems. Writers who have found their "voice" listen to the particular song inside themselves and bring it forth. Elisabeth once said her only real fear is not death, but that she won't find a way to express who she is in the world. Maybe her expression will involve some form of return to the songs that flowed freely from her heart as a child.

> From immemorial times the inspiring effect of
> the invisible sound that moves all hearts, and draws
> them together, has mystified mankind.
>
> —*I Ching*

Buy yourself a harmonica. All it takes to make beautiful sound is your breathing. Or sit at a piano, grab a guitar, use any surface as a drum. Make spontaneous music that comes from your heart. Socrates himself was advised by his "daemon" (his muse or guide), "You ought to make more music." Give yourself time alone, where no one can hear you.

Make up a song for a child, grandchild, or pet. When my kids were babies I made up a simple lullaby for each of them. Just singing their name over and over to a little tune will do. Start with a hum and let the sound wander. A tune will likely come to you. If not, borrow one. A friend made up a song for her baby to the tune of "Edelweiss." Let it be simple, one or two notes.

Emulate Winnie the Pooh, who often felt "a hum" coming on. Put a few words to the hum. Sing it when you're driving or walking. No one has to hear, although you might want to sing it to someone you love. Make up a song for someone dying. Sing it to him or her. Dying people aren't judgmental.

Poppa's cousin Ruthie approaches the world through song and is most proud of the songs she wrote to her husband when he was dying. Next she loves the song she wrote as a tribute to Poppa's flamboyant and passionate aunt Anne, who always wore a flower in her hair and was forever marching for a cause. She's been known as Uncle Ruthie on her radio show in L.A. for years. Poppa called her Cousin Uncle Ruthie. When I first met her in Chicago years ago, I was on my way to a workshop and commented, "Oh, drat, my harmonica is plugged up." Cousin Uncle Ruthie reached into her bag and said, "Here, take mine. It's an extra."

Ruthie says she just lets songs arrive. Singer-songwriter Neil Young said in an interview, "If an idea comes to me I see it as a gift and roll with the muse. I'm faithful to that one thing. All of this is coming from somewhere. I just have to stand there with open arms. That's what has brought me success. If the muse calls I drop everything and go with it."

> Remember the lips
> where the wind-breath originated,
> and let your note be clear.
> Don't try to end it.
> *Be your note* . . .
> Sing loud!
>
> —RUMI

35

···

the undersong

·

Even now in the middle of the night if I wake,
as I often do, I hear the night . . . a sound
that seems to emanate from the movement
of the spheres. It's coming from me . . .
Listen! We make a world! I hear the sound
of matter pouring through eternal forms.
—STANLEY KUNITZ

Our brains are hungry for the new. Time and again I watch words in random patterns shift people into another realm. Words can take us to a river of soul, connecting to our unconscious in ways I can't explain, tapping in to a rushing undersong, a passionate realm holding letters of the alphabet, song, sounds, the meaning of everything. And kids, especially, dive into the hushed current.

I wonder if this river runs through the land of the right brain or the frontal lobe. I wonder if this is what the kabbalistic rabbis were working with at night, in white robes, by candlelight, conjuring the divine. According to David Abrams in *The Spell of the Sensuous*, the Hebrew scribes never lost this sense of the letters as living, animate powers. The Kabbalah centered around the conviction that each of the twenty-two letters of the Hebrew *aleph-beth* is a magic gateway or guide into an entire sphere of existence.

I often suggest that people spin before they write, to loosen up. In a workshop in Pleasanton, California, one day, we did a lot of spinning. "I feel the need to write upside down," one child, age ten, said solemnly. She wrote *upside down* in red pen, upside down. Gathering words from books of poetry, someone tossed out *Kronalaga,* a place, and then our word, *undersong.* We begin to define *undersong,* and the poems that day carried the meaning we spun into the word. That same ten-year-old girl closed her poem

> I come from a planet of upside down CDs.
> I will come to consciousness . . .
> The night says come,
> the poet in Kronalaga is spinning. . . .

The undersong lives in us at any age. In Red Bluff, California, an elderly woman joined a workshop late and frazzled. She began, "I am tired and confused . . ." When she moved to *come forth,* a refrain suggested as a prompt, she began, "Come forth energy and clear-mindedness, come forth farsightedness. . . . Come forth redwood island," and soon her writing shifted. She began to look younger and composed. She gathered tickets to play with words and wrote, "One afternoon when running wild/ with a ribbon flowing from my hair/ I was given seven choices/ 1) the wisdom of the ocean/ 2) the knowledge of the sun/ 3) the energy of flowers/ 4) the art of tiny pieces/ 5) the aura of the moon/ 6) the key to another long thought/ 7) another chance."

This all came forth after she asked, in a written invocation, for energy and insight. The response in the form of a poem emerged from the undersong through our wordpool and the word tickets. In another workshop we had a lively time creating a wordpool centered on wishes, music, the earth, war, peace, love, and the mystery of who we are. A ten-year-old girl, caught in the rush of words and the rhythm of the undersong, wrote (I've kept her spelling)

> I wish I was a perfect rysym flowing from music to music,
> suddenly, a blossom blooms in the cold damp winter,
> like a handful of mericals that dropped down on Earth.
> I am waters of friendly spirits,
> no wars can fool the great water,
> only love can fool me.

An eight-year-old girl wrote, "Today I am love and a spontaneous milky way filled with questions."

And a six-year-old wrote, "I love the dim moon. . . . I love the immense kindness."

Although it won't make the news, the undersong is brimming with an upwelling of soul and spirit just below the surface, tumbling out alive in our children and elders, hidden in everyone. Sit quietly and see if you can feel it; allow a sense of the undersong to inform your own writing.

36

....

nichtalelloudi:
would you be willing

.

He went hiding into the garden of night flowers.
—ODYSSEUS ELYTIS

You may feel like a *nichtalelloudi*, a night flower that opens in moonlight when it's safe, when you might even be asleep, sneaking up on yourself in dreams. I tell this to the kids (ages twelve to eighteen) on my first day in the Juvenile Hall school this spring. I write the Greek word *nichtalelloudi* on the board with an orange pen.

At that first session, twelve-year-old André didn't write. (André is not his real name. I've changed all the students' names in this chapter.) He sat with his head on the desk beside a teacher named Sally and cried. A lovable, lanky boy, André has bright eyes and wild, curly hair. Before you feel too sorry for him, Luisa, the teacher, tells me, understand that he's the kind of kid who rides up to you in the park on a bike holding a knife, saying, "Give me whatever you've got."

I can feel sorry that he hasn't been given the language of poetry yet.

At the second session, André feels safer when he sees his friends' poems treated equally with no judgment. Emphasizing "I come from," he writes (with Sally's help along with word tickets and our wordpool on the board)

> I come from the soul of fire
> My heart says there are rings of chances
> My soul is suddenly traveling in the lights of time
> It seems like my soul is visiting a place that it has never been
>   before

André has never been to the world of poetry, where night flowers bloom in hidden safety and where he might need to live. At the next session, we talk about aspects of "nonviolent" or "compassionate" communication (as taught by Marshall Rosenberg). First allow your feeling to come forth and express it. Next, figure out and say what you need. Third, request (but don't demand) what you want: "Would you be willing?"

I add the option of "bring me."

André writes

> I feel like late-afternoon light
> I am a flight of thunder canyons
> Bring me an arctic snowgoose on its flight home

Would you be willing to call another breathtaking
spring day of rain and snow
We could take a sleepwalk on the clouds

At our fourth session, André still wants *nichtalelloudi* on the
board. All he's been thinking about, he says, is *nichtalelloudi*. It's a
threshold to poetry for him. Most likely André feels he's too much.
Even his name, André (French, with an *accent aigu*), is foreign
sounding, like *nichtalelloudi*.

An Eskimo word for poetry, I've read, also means "to
breathe." I ask my poet friend Bob who he'd be without poetry.
"Dead," he says. Maybe André needs poetry that much. His behavior might be leading to his death (and that of others). In most workshops I find both kids and adults hungry for what poetry brings.

At that fourth session we talk about feelings. The often
buzzing room is totally quiet when I say, "Maybe your feelings are
so huge you don't know what to do with them. Your feelings are
so out-of-bounds and passionate they get you in trouble.

"It takes courage," I hear myself say—coeur*age*, "with
heart"—to stop and sense what we're truly feeling and then to express it. It's courageous to go farther, figure out and express what
we need. And maybe it's most courageous of all to ask for what we
want: "Would you be willing?" I've read that courage is literally
"a rage of the heart," compassion meeting righteous anger leading
to nonviolent action.

Carlita, hair pulled tight back over olive skin, dark eyes
looking masked, is the toughest kid in the Hall, I'm told. "You
should see her do pushups," Luisa says. Carlita won't write on that

fourth day. There's been a fight. Tension is high. Everyone's unusually quiet. Gang boundaries have been crossed and she's in the middle of it. Physical boundaries in the Hall are marked by wide yellow tape kids can't step past.

Leaning beside Carlita at her desk, I ask what she's feeling. "Angry," she says finally, disdainful. Anger usually hides another feeling, I suggest. Is it sadness? She silently agrees and I sense her soften just a bit. I ask her to define the feeling. How big is it?

"How do you measure sadness?" She snaps. "Can I write that down?" I ask, and (with permission) write her words, "How do you measure sadness?" We work together until she's ready (with word tickets: *tented, windshield, piles of sand, canyons*) to write on her own. Then we read her poem aloud to the group.

I feel like neverending anger. . . .
My sadness inside grows with each passing day.
How do you measure the canyons of emotions hidden deep?
The tented windshield to my eyes
is a barrier so no one can see inside.
Piles of sand have filled my soul.
There is yellow caution tape surrounding my heart. . . .

After this, somehow feeling safer expressing her feelings, Carlita writes poem after poem.

Jay, an Asian gang leader, wants someone to ask who he is beyond stereotype. He wants the safety and beauty of his true nature to be known, both by himself and by the outside world. And he needs the nourishment of nature's rivers. Maybe he needs a river of words, small, yet endlessly expressive.

> I feel like a miracle musical sofa.
> I am a million winter lifts
> because I need an escape
> from life's mistakes.

> Bring me award-winning ground where stars appear.
> Would you be willing?
> Would you be willing
> to ask who I am?

> Would you be willing
> to be a king?
> Because I need small rivers to drink.

It's a delight to write in a tongue that matches the uniqueness of our spirit. Working in the Juvenile Hall, I'm reminded again and again that although daring, risk, and wildness are part of creativity, the opposite is also crucial, especially for those of us who feel fragile. To express the vastness of who we are, to write about and shape our feelings, a sense of safety can be essential. The safety of no judgment becomes *una puerta*. A door. In both Spanish and English we read these words from Vicente Huidobro's poem "Ars Poetica."

> Que el verso sea como una llave
> Que abra mil puertas

Let poetry be like a key
Opening a thousand doors

IN THE SAFETY of your journal or with friends, examine what you're feeling. Create a wordpool to begin to express it. Gather books of poems and steal single words, not phrases. Gather words at random, sloppily, aslant, in circles, even upside down on a page. Use every color pen or pencil. Open with "I feel" and use some of the words you've gathered. Begin to examine what need your feelings reveal. Write more lines opening with "Because I need," also using stolen words. Soon they'll be yours. Words—I remind people again and again—are free. Write this to yourself or to someone in your life. Form a request opening more lines with the words "Would you be willing."

Look into Marshall Rosenberg's work (and books) on nonviolent communication. Play with this. Write in the middle of the night when you can't sleep. Whenever you can, write in moonlight. You might find that you begin to glow.

A mind that is lively and inquiring, compassionate,
curious, angry, full of music, full of feeling,
is a mind full of possible poetry.
Poetry is a life-cherishing force. . . . For poems
are not words, after all, but fires for the cold, ropes let
down to the lost, something as necessary as bread in the
pockets of the hungry.
—MARY OLIVER

37

....

zomoli

·

A single kernel of energy could have become
everything that is. A lot happened in the first
second of time . . . all contained in a tiny spark
of energy ruled by a single primordial law.
—STEPHEN HAWKING

A man is as vast as he acts
—MESSAGE ON A YOGI TEA BAG

Night flowers are closing as the
moon disappears and geese lift out of soaked rice fields on an early
spring morning as I drive to San Francisco. A great blue heron angles high above the road and egrets pose like skinny ice statues in
roadside ditches. I'm in the buoyant mood that often comes over
me on the road.

I've been talking about writing with my friend Jane, who
says the word *creativity* bothers her. She calls it *generativity*. But

that's a mouthful for me, too cold and Latin. The word *expressiveness* doesn't do it, either. No heart or hum. I've been searching for the right word that might well be floating nearby in a language I don't know. Here on the road I decide to come up with a word or phrase of my own.

Kokoro means heart, mind, and soul in Japanese. Playing with words in a Pleasanton workshop once, we added *spirit* and *body* and made up an extended word, *kokorospibo*—heart, mind, soul, spirit, and body.

Now I want a word that holds *kokorospibo* as well as the Greek word for night flower, *nichtalelloudi.* And joy. No small task.

I want this word to encompass the living seed as well as its protective husk or container. It contains an intense, condensed germ so minute as to be immeasurable, and the heart of it (although also watery) includes a bright spark. It will embrace both light and dark, masculine and feminine, yin and yang. The word must synthesize opposites and edges.

I want a word so large and full of life as it spirals through our imagination that the universe and thus all our ideas emerge from it. That's all I want!

And the spark it defines must live within it, like *zomoli.* Yes, here it is. *Zomoli.*

Let's give the word a chance. I simply invited a new word and *zomoli* kind of floated into me in this landscape filled with birds startling out of grasses in a shifting field (like an exaltation of larks). I might have started with *zoom,* a word I love, *zoomoli.* It sounds like another word I love, *momoli,* which is Native American Maidu for water, or "voice of a living spring."

Zomoli opens, by chance, with the *ʒo* of *ʒoe*, "life," in Greek. Also, by chance, *ʒomoli* has part of *moon,* and *om,* and the simplicity of *homily, home, Mom,* and a slight ring of the word *holy. Zomoli.* There's even the o . . . ol of *fool.* The letter *ʒ* brings energetic zaniness, dream questing, foolishness, and *Yetʒer Ha Rah*—a concept within Judaism (notice the *ʒ*) reminding us that the divine includes the outlaw, rascal, outrageousness, laughter, danger.

Zomoli. Why not?

Zomoli. Orderly and chaotic, like the sea at Shell Beach.

I wonder if zomoli—embracing opposites to invoke something new, a synthesis—has an opposite itself. My doubting self wonders if I've earned the word. Thou shalt not create a new word. Who the hell dost thou think thou art? Hell may well be *thou shalt.* Aha, maybe this is the opposite of zomoli.

Zomoli is both a spark and a field. It's the liveliness inside each of us, whirring, that we'll never quite understand. It's microscopic and vast and invisible all at once, complicated and simple, like we are, both silly and serious, encompassing *(en compass sing)* paradox and play, circling at the heart of it.

MAKE UP YOUR OWN WORD. When Chilean poet Gonzalo Rojas heard his brother say *relampago* for "lightning" while it hailed on their zinc roof, he was mesmerized by the word. "Since then," Rojas said, "I have lived in the zumbido, the buzzing of words" (from John Oliver Simon's introduction to his translation of *The Velocities of the Possible* by Rojas).

What have you been unable to express? Maybe an aspect of your personality no one understands or a concept you'd like to redefine? Mess around with letters and sounds you like, borrowing from foreign languages. A different world view is encoded in the words. *Helio,* "sun" in Greek. *Munmunum,* "mugwort" in Maidu. Hum different words, turn them around, play with opposites. Scan a dictionary. Reinvent or spin off a word that's new to you. Tumble it. Where the heck do our words come from, anyhow?

Don't think too hard. Just invite a word to come and visit. For fun. My friend Vince made up the word *proaquen* for whatever we want it to mean.

Read "Jabberwocky" by Lewis Carroll: "'Twas brillig, and the slithy toves/ Did gyre and gimble in the wabe:/ All mimsy were the borogoves,/ and the mome raths outgrabe." Lewis Carroll is said to have added more words to the English language than any other writer.

Make up a word for the love you want to give and receive in your life. Make up a word for where you're going, because no one has ever been there before, to help you, in Emily Dickinson's words, "tell all the truth and tell it slant."

A language has to be found—for that matter,
every word being an idea, the time of the universal
language will come! . . . This new language would be of
the soul, for the soul, containing everything, smells,
sounds, colors; thought latching on
to thought and pulling.
—ARTHUR RIMBAUD

38

write crazy love poems

·

Always be a poet, even in prose.
—CHARLES BAUDELAIRE

There's someone out there who needs you. Live
your life so that person can find you.
—BALINESE DANCER

When I was sixteen, brilliant,
brooding Richard B. sat next to me in high school English. We both
loved words. He'd pencil words on flaps of envelopes and slip
them to me under the desk: "She held the frailest winds in her arms,
and her toes, which danced, were stars." A hip, sexy, edgy import
from the juvenile detention system with a James Dean attitude and
tight jeans, Richard also snuck notes to me in German class: "German is a 'glomerate of gutterals and belchery, a quarter-irritation in
the belly of a vocal cord." I taped his irreverent, beat notes into my
journal. And sure enough, I fell for him.

Poetry wins hearts. When I first dated Kent, he recited an Ezra Pound poem to me on a picnic and wrote the final lines into my journal for me, "And I would rather have my sweet, though rose leaves die of grieving, / than do high deeds in Hungary to pass all men's believing."

I've never forgotten that poem or that moment engaging my heart, lounging with Kent on the grass. He's the man I married. As time passes since our divorce, I think we're both remembering our happier years with love of poetry, language, and each other. We confide in each other about matters of love. Do I have to follow "the Rules"? I want to know. He called recently, pacing, asking if I could visit and talk to him about a current potential breakup. They worked it out. I'll have to ask what he suggests I do with the emergence of two appealing suitors at once.

I wrote Kent a few love poems, but I'm not sure I ever showed him. This little rhyming almost-love poem I remember by heart: "I know your hands/ how they hold things./ Your uncut diamond core/ that I have always sought./ Your walk and your hollows/ more than I ever thought./ And it follows/ that you know me/ my doubt, my small displays/ my ceaseless in and out/ and my Arabian night ways . . ."

If I didn't, I wish I had shown these words to Kent. For years I didn't show my poems to anyone. Now I wonder if revealing my poems, my feelings, and my vulnerability might have shifted the course of our marriage. Maybe not. Maybe Kent and I were together just the right amount of time.

Although it might make us feel vulnerable, we can either

·

write our own poems or we can find poems by others that express feelings for us and memorize them or send them into the world to someone we love. Samuel Taylor Coleridge might have the words you need one day: "Beware, beware his flashing eyes/ his floating hair/ draw a circle round him thrice/ and close your eyes with holy dread/ for he on honeydew hath fed/ and drunk the milk of paradise."

Writing, reciting, or sending love poems can help us both see and be what we're looking for in love. Maybe "the" person will appear in our lives to catch the poem in midair. Maybe the person we're with will *become* who we need when we give him or her our poems.

AUTHOR GAY HENDRICKS SUGGESTS that we compose a hundred sentences revealing both who we want to be in a relationship and what we would like to offer a partner, not just what we wish for and need ourselves. Why not dive within and then call and dream forth love, beginning with words, free, playful, wild? When I wrote the following rambling invocation, I put down whatever spilled out with no judgment or control, just wild word flinging. You can shape things later if you want, cutting whatever you've heard before or whatever doesn't ring true.

Steal words from the world around you, not necessarily related to love. I form images by looking at what's around me. Word tickets or words gathered from books of poems are helpful: *river-hills, lackadaisical, sorcery*. Play with your words if you want a playful lover.

I started with a little nonsense Spanish/Italian.

Mi esposito, mi cumpleaños, mi colores! Mi paparazzi! Mi papparazzouli!

I shifted to heroes and loves.

Mi Gandhi Lisa, redwood forest, blue waves. I love your wanton soups, mi Don Quixote, Che Guevara Depp-man, mi lost in translation big bill laugher, story telling slow dance salsa samba god swinger.

On to native Maidu words.

Mi munmunum, momoli, simpoko, pompoko.

And more heroes.

Mi Michelangelo, Einstein capoeira guy. Mi soft rain thunder man in the god's eye

Then I move to a "come to me" refrain.

Come to me! Fly to me, laugh dance sing write to me, mi leafy jungle guy. Yes! I say yes! A long low Molly Bloom far flung farfignugen yes!

And then I swing to what I offer.

·

I bring you branches. Chocolates. I bring you my koko-rospibo, zomoli world maker. I bring you underground soups. And kisses, whirlpooling around your secrets of water. You glint on them with your sun. I bring you mysteries of stone you wash with soul water. Our invisible chambers meet.

Finally I shift to who we are together.

We're the walls of Machu Picchu, Stonehenge lichens, light through solstice portal, flames bending to meet. Laughing, hilarious. We're owl poems alive with night, cougars loping, god-glazed buttercups in a hidden glade. We're the shade, the snake, dragon, rabbit, wild parrots spinning outside of time. We write crazy love poems. We *are* crazy love poems.

Now, just for fun, write your own crazy love poems. Write to the people you love to expand your idea of who they might be or to invoke your new lover, the person you know your love will be. Write as the person you most truly are—and are continually be-coming.

Place poems as want ads. For fun once, although I never placed it anywhere, I wrote an ad with images from a dream.

VALENTINE PERSONAL

One woman, three cougars in the dining room, bear in the kitchen lighting fires, one woman shifting, in the ocean, in the long rain, under a silk hood, come alive, waiting for a man who loves cougars, bears, fires, ocean, life.

Sometimes you might want to be real and believable in your writing, serene and grounded and calmly loving. Other times, go bananas. Do this in the middle of the night. Do this in the rain. Do this burning candles. Do this perched on a balcony like Rapunzel. Let your hair down. Weep and laugh for love. Run the lines together. Rant, spin, dash outside to ask the trees for help, and write more. Be a lover in a fairy tale that ends happily ever after.

Then, look out. Be ready to dive in, or to run.

And in the meantime, love the people around you and those who come your way.

> In order to create there must be a dynamic force, and
> what force is more potent than love?
> —IGOR STRAVINSKY

39

underground soup

·

Claire always believed her ship would come in
the day she learned to make soups.

—S.W.

My son, Dan, began dreaming
and daydreaming soups when he worked in the kitchen at Chico
Natural Foods. He first created his Aztec Soup in memory of his
grandpa Julian, who loved pre-Columbian art. Dan's soup was a
love tribute to Poppa in food form, a love food. In the novel *Like
Water for Chocolate*, by Laura Esquivel, meals are created as magic
potions. To the Chinese, food is medicine. Increasingly, it also
seems to me, food is seen as art.

The base of Dan's Aztec Soup is quinoa, an ancient Aztec
grain. His recipe includes red and green peppers, corn, yams, and
onions. Another soup Dan refined from a recipe in a daydream
was white bean and black olive.

I believe in soups. "Hot Soup," a story I wrote years ago

about a woman named Claire in a prison romance, centered on a pot of homemade soup. Dan helped my soups (and increased the fun of cooking) by suggesting that if ingredients look good—with balanced colors, shapes, and sizes—the food is more likely to taste good. Colors also herald a rich variety of vitamins and minerals.

Preparing soup after Thanksgiving, I dabbed in flavors of color. I floated squares of yam (rich orange rust). I sprinkled in a fistful of dried cranberries (dots of magenta—no, indeed, cranberry red). I stirred in green strips of kale, shaved orange carrot circles along with thin rings of onion and pale curves of celery. Normally I rush my cooking, but for this soup I noticed the shape, color, and texture of each vegetable. Last I spooned in leftover creamy mashed potatoes and what remained of the stuffing. I even poured in honey-colored gravy. At the beginning and end I snipped in parsley with my orange kitchen scissors.

Preparing this soup was slow and playful, almost like writing a poem. The soup was beautiful, nutritious, and delicious. My best ever, Dan thinks.

Recently I concocted what I call Underground Soup for Elisabeth, who was recovering from the flu, based on our personal joke/ love vegetable, the beet. Most of the ingredients grow under the ground with hidden color. Again I pretend I'm an artist as I sauté one large red onion, a white onion, and a yellow onion in olive oil. I dice two or three scrubbed heart-shaped beets into chunky triangles, turning the soup a lush magenta. Slim rounds from five or six organic carrots float like orange suns reflected in a beet-pink sea. Half-moons from a turnip add translucent white boats, along with a flotilla of five or six radishes sliced in half-moons. I sliver half of a red cabbage in curly curves. Now the soup needs green. I scissor in vibrant snippets of kale or chard and parsley; toss in flame raisins that fatten into sweet, wrinkly spheres; sprinkle in sea salt and several shakes of balsamic vinegar. Chunks of pumpkin-orange yam are optional.

I simmer all this in a large pot about one third full of water, adding more parsley at the end for green. The fuchsia soup is lovely served hot or cold in blue bowls with fresh parsley or dill topping white dollops of whole-milk yogurt. It reminds me of its cool cousin, borscht.

A soup, like a book and its chapters, I think, is made of discrete parts that merge into a whole yet keep their individual flavor and character, not too crunchy, not too mushy. We work to stir the whole together, spiraling words or matzoh balls or carrots with a wooden spoon. We're warmed by soups, nourished, brought together around heartening sustenance for our other creative soul work as well.

LUNCH

The bread and what may sleep between,
translucent cucumber, sweet butter,
mustard from the mustard seed,
cracking yellow kernel of faith,
and the drink, the balm,
the lips, swallowing,
the world is an incredible feast
and all we need is an appetite.

—S.W.

APPROACH COOKING like a painter. Pretend foods are paints on a palette. Play with color and texture. Shop as if you're choosing watercolors or acrylics. If you don't want to go to the store, make soup using what's in the fridge, even if it's limp, lifeless, half gone. Sprouting carrots, pale celery, a lone, slighted turnip. Bring it to life with contrasting colors. Add raisins. A bit of apple. Green or purple grapes. Play with what you find. Forage outside and clip or pinch anything green in your garden, summer fall winter spring. Go for wild lamb's-quarter (rich in calcium). Purslane. Wild dock. Toss in rose petals, nasturtiums, calendula. I live in California, where I can always gather rosemary, oregano, mint, sage, and often chives. Paint with them. Serve in large, colorful bowls. Feel yourself turn Technicolor inside.

> Creative expression is not only alive in our major
> projects, but also present in the normal course of
> everyday life—how we organize our work space
> or our home, how we prepare our meals,
> or even how we structure our time.
> —CAROLINE MYSS

40

strawberries

·

We must risk delight.
—JACK GILBERT

When they're sliced in half and sideways, I notice, strawberries look like narrow eyes with long, white-pink lashes. Slice one and see. Look at the world sideways, they suggest, with different eyes. Climb up a hill in your imagination and watch yourself and the people you know through your heart.

I photograph strawberry twin hearts. Then I eat them, almost waiting to hear Miriam Makeba singing, "Strawwwwwwwberries, love tastes like strawberries." Each berry heart, I notice, has another long, pale, thin heart in the center, with lines radiating out like beams of light toward the surface, where every seed is a tiny yellow planet. The heart isn't always hidden, I see. The strawberry is the heart outright, red and fragile, seeds sweet in the skin like sandy pores.

The poet Fernando Pessoa longs to think and write with an open heart like the flowers (and strawberries) but can't express himself as they do, stating in a poem, "Because I lack the divine simplicity/ to be all on the outside only." And the poet Jorge Argueta writes about how happy it makes him to bite such a gentle heart as the strawberry "that carries in its center/ another heart."

41

artist of plants

·

Who was this man who found happiness strolling
about chanting poems like a careless sage and
penetrating the mysteries of bamboo?
—Su Shih about Yu Ko, China, 1070

The Creamsicle-orange shirt on
a portly man behind me in line at Upper Crust Café makes me
crave something sweet. Reading my mind, the man urges me to
order cherry cheesecake instead of salad. I stubbornly resist, but
soon find him perched at the table next to my writing corner with
his glistening slice.

As I nibble salad dutifully, he informs me he's a gardener
named Ben. He likes to dig up rocks on his land, especially jade.
When he looks at the earth, he confides, he can visualize what will
be underground where he digs. My mind wanders to wondering if
Poppa could see underground in his foraging for feldspar, calcite.

He never would have said it, unwilling to acknowledge in himself or others abilities not recognized by modern science.

When Ben asks what I'm writing, I explain that today I've been describing my son's day-dreamed soups, pondering different ways we can be artists—in the kitchen, for example.

"I call myself an artist of plants," Ben muses when I ask about his gardening. "I look at a small plant and see what it will look like grown up. I tore up all my grass and set down cobblestones for my mind. I visualize wildflowers coming up through stones: garden asters, veronicas, cushion mums, dwarf daylilies, red yarrow—plants under twelve inches. Behind that, bigger plants like ruby glow and coreopsis and then larger grandifloras like roses. I just dug an unwanted President Lincoln red rose from someone's yard. Behind all that, river birch.

"I'll have dogwoods and Japanese maples on the west, and varieties of daylily. I'm going to get big rocks—limestone boulders, jadeite, and ruffle betroitle," he adds with a mischievous grin.

"Ruffle betroitle! How do you spell it?" I ask. We guess, and I confess that my gardens all end up wild; colorful but unruly. Now the mint's taking over, along with Santa Barbara daisies, lamb's ear, artemesia, and violets. I read somewhere that people's gardens tell a lot about who they are.

Ben enjoys talking as I jot his remarks into my journal. Since he sees I'm a lowly writer, no lofty artist of plants, Ben doesn't want to leave me bereft. Grateful for my interest in his garden, he offers me the last bite of his shimmering cheesecake and says, kindly, thoughtfully, "You're an artist, too, with people."

I thank him, savoring my creamy bite, and wondering, hmm,

if it's time to forget this writing business. Maybe I need to spend more time with flowers and herbs and vegetables. I love the silvery sages. A writer friend recently e-mailed, "The earth is my favorite medium at the moment . . . weeding and seeding."

I have other friends who are artists of plants who choose colors in bloom cycles, contrast textures and heights, balance round redbud leaves with silver spears of sage. Soft lamb's ear brushes against their angular boulders. By shaping spaces—I'm hiring Cheryl to help me—you can make a series of rooms in a garden. Another friend has created a room-size ceremonial labyrinth just behind her house. My neighbor Mandy just set a lotus plant— sacred in both India and Egypt—near the pathway to our houses. It basks in a giant green pot pond. Two plate-size lotus leaves with vein spokes seem to float on my coffee table.

Poppa sloped daffodils from the dunes house like a spilling creek of yellow. An artist fashioned a Japanese garden in Mom and Poppa's Chicago yard with large black pumice lava rocks for accents. I found it stark at first, but it softened as things grew. Poppa added weathered limestone statues salvaged from old buildings draped with delicate ivy against used red-brick garden walls. He set large crystal-laden rocks among the salvia, ajuga, daylilies, and a flowering hawthorn tree where Kent and I were married.

Because I often find large spaces overwhelming, I create imaginary gardens in small boxes. Recently I gathered a handful of trampled, frayed eucalyptus leaves showing veins and spine like people worn to nerve and bone. The last box I made looks like a glimpse of oddly symmetrical forest floor. The boxes become microcosms of wherever we put them together.

For Ben, fashioning a living garden helps him feel he can direct his world. He can imaginatively fill it with what his life needs, taking him deep inside nature and himself in an orderly, changing field of color, fragrance, oxygen, and light, inviting bees, mantises, children, deer, and birds.

> One of the great satisfactions of the human spirit is to
> feel that one's family extends across the borders of the
> species and belongs to everything that lives. And one
> has the same feeling about the flowers and plants in
> general and shrubs and trees, that they all belong
> to your family. That makes one feel more kindred
> than if you're isolated in your species.
> —STANLEY KUNITZ

IF YOU DON'T HAVE A YARD OR GARDEN, fill a terrarium or a window box, like my friend Joann's rows of blossoming shamrock in the windows of her Manhattan loft. Arrange pebbles of different size and color at the base of a large plant. Get those fingers in the dirt. Grow cherry tomatoes in a summer window. Buy yourself a bonsai tree. At least keep a vase of flowers on your table, or a stolen gardenia pinched from a neighborhood bush. And tape pressed petals, Creamsicle orange, cherry cheesecake pink, into your blossoming journal—one hidden petal from the center of a rose.

Make a miniature garden in a box. Copy it in a micro-garden in a large pot or small area of greeting outside your front door. Let yourself feel like an artist of whatever you love to do, whether or not it has anything to do with growing things.

When my artist friend Franziska remarked one day, "Keeping house is so creative," I noticed that she infuses every area of her life with her playful and colorful way of seeing; her dress, home, and meals as well as her garden. Although dust bunnies may be present, every surface, wall, room, shoe, soup, and sentence is open for playful transformation. Franziska made a life-size doll and traveled with "Mrs. Meyer" in the front seat of her car, just for fun.

Think of areas of life to approach as an artist. Some people are artists of hair, enhancing our faces. Some people's art is diplomacy, decorating, entertaining. If you want, allow yourself to begin to bring color, contrast, light—and flowers—to everything you do.

When I knit, as when I write, I find myself in ecstatic
participation in a divinely animated world.
—BERNADETTE MURPHY

42

entering the blue

·

I find that if I don't give shape to my experience
in language, if I don't spend time in the crafting
and honing of that experience in words,
I don't feel real to myself. It's as if the layer of
experience which completes myself is the act of
writing, the act of naming what I've known.
—MARK DOTY

My mom might have water on
the brain. We're in Chicago, wondering why her walking has become an erratic stumble. It's almost as if her body is abandoning
her. Mom's hair is still almost all brown. Sometimes she looks like
an aging child. She has the determination of a little girl taking her
first steps, stubbornly deliberate, willful. Lots of people, I argue,
lurch or dodder or wheel about Montgomery Place, a retirement
community where Mom has an apartment overlooking Lake
Michigan. When Poppa was near death, I promised him Mom

would be safe without him. Was this true? How can I keep her safe? We lie in bed together a lot and talk and laugh like kids at a slumber party.

I've been walking along lakeside rocks on a peninsula called "the point" each day with my journal, jotting notes on my way to swim. I don't remember Lake Michigan being aquamarine, both Mom's and my favorite color. I settle on the same flat rock where I spread my towel as a teen and slither again through waves slapping a tumble of chunky boulders. I've swum here three times this visit, opening my eyes in blue lake light.

Back at Mom's apartment, I read aloud, "Atypical normal pressure hydrocephalus. Isn't that a contradiction in terms? Atypical normal?"

"Yes," Mom agrees, busy with unruly mail. "But, well, that's what I have," she says. "I don't know. Everyone finds something different wrong with me." Sometimes I wonder if Mom has ever fully inhabited her body. And to me it seems that when Poppa died she abandoned it further. And all the unwept tears traveled to the top of her head like a storm cloud. But that's just my idea. All Mom's difficulties are motor; she seems as sharp as ever. Her once-flowing handwriting trails into small scribbles and soon she'll need a scribe. I've been recording donations for her, an important part of her idea of who she is, and paying some of the bills.

Mom and I are organizing her piles of mail, almost as unruly as my emotions, which shift from sadness to anger, to love, to fear of abandonment, to silly giggling with Mom, who, in many ways, over the years, has become my best friend

Now we stare out her thirteenth-floor window toward the

Fifty-seventh Street Beach and the Museum of Science and Industry. "There's a lot for me to watch," Mom says. "I look for birds, cars, how many people are on the beach and if the lifeguard's there. See? There he is. At night I watch airplanes coming down. When Elisabeth was here the wind was in the wrong direction. They weren't coming."

"The next major accomplishment is to get into the bed," Mom says. "I plop in and pull myself over. Unfortunately this headboard isn't very strong." She's angling in for a nap. "And God knows what's under the bed . . ."

"Cremation society," I read, lifting an envelope from her drawer as we sort through letters and accumulated papers. "That's something to keep over there," she says, pointing toward the credenza on the far wall.

"You told me to keep instructions," she adds. "They're in the dresser drawer to the right." Instructions for cremation?

"You're giving me more chapters," I say, jotting notes.

"Do you need more chapters?" Mom wants to know, and adds, "You do what you like to do, don't you?" Yes, I say, understanding that most of Mom's life has been dedicated to doing things for other people. She's unable to do that now.

As we talk and I scrawl down her words, I realize that indeed, my current practice seems to be gathering words into chapters, hundreds like this that ease toward me like the current in Chico Creek or come at me choppy, like waves, like this rush of emotions I feel around Mom, swirling about my heart. I do my best to chisel chapters into usable blocks like the limestone at the point sunk into the lake, seemingly bottomless at the edges, where

I slip in from green moss. I guess the chapters help me wrestle emotions into shape. Frame them.

Chapters make things manageable, with a distinct beginning and ending. I can open them and I can close them. Life is a wild out-of-control flowing force. A piece of it can almost be held in place by a chapter. (Like a photo, poem, song, collage box, page in a journal.) The writing shifts me to a larger, safer, more impersonal world where everything, no matter how difficult, can be held in place, made more sensible and sometimes more beautiful—whittled, painted, spun by imagination.

I hold up a blue plastic flashlight.

"I keep that by the bed," Mom says. "Why?" I ask. "That's where you're supposed to keep them," she insists. I ask about a Porter, Indiana, fire department plastic key chain from the drawer I'm arranging, and then toss it. Mom says, "You're throwing my life away." "Mom!" I say, loud, only half believing myself, "You're not these name badges gathered in the drawer! You're Ethel Goldsmith with or without these name badges!"

"We need this yellow card," she insists, pulling a 1950s Civil Defense Preparedness air raid preparation card from my grasp. "It's worth something now." It's about crouching under desks when sirens blast three times, a bit out of date in Mom's collection of instructions, though not as out of date as I'd like it to be. I set it next to Grandpapa Mitch's 1940s business card. Maybe I'll put all this into a Chicago collage.

The next morning I decide to swim at the beach, since I'm leaving in the afternoon and we're short on time. It's hard for me to leave Mom in Chicago, but she's adamant about staying here for now. The lifeguard is out rowing and clusters of people wade at the edge of the water in a cold spot. They haven't found the warm area where I slosh in with the breaststroke.

Walking back, I wave up at Mom's window even though she's not standing where I usually see her, waving both arms back. I feel a rush of loss. She's napping. Besides, it's increasingly difficult for her to make it to the window. What are we going to do? I jot notes into my journal for solace. Sometimes on walks I call from my cell phone to tell Mom I'm in view. She watched me running on the beach two nights ago, recognizing my orange, green, and blue skirt. She didn't know I was singing "The Girl from Ipanema" as I splashed at the edge of the water, thinking about each of us, in our own way, together, entering the blue.

MY FEELINGS SHIFT when I write about something. Piecing this chapter together helped me with my sadness at Mom's decline while I was with her last week. When I observe, record, and shape an experience it becomes more impersonal and universal. Writing my way through things helps me both make sense out of an experience and remove myself from some of the grief and intensity. It's paradoxical. Writing makes me more present, more fully there, observing closely, and at the same time, one step removed. It's easier to laugh about things when I'm slightly detached. Maybe I float off in the protective bubble of so-called art.

Surely there's something brewing in your life that needs to be acknowledged in a chapter or an essay—something you want to hold together, save, or transmute. One of my friends said recently that he had suffered and suffered about something. Then he wrote it down and it was gone.

Carry your journal and begin writing "on the spot" like a reporter. Look over chapters or essays you read and notice how the writer shaped experience. Notice where the writer began and how the writer ended.

What's breaking your heart? What does your heart have to say about it? Notice how your heart wants you to begin and end what you write. How would your heart change things if it could? Describe the landscape of your heart right now. Where would your heart most like to take you? Where is it most afraid to go? How does writing about this shift the way your heart feels in your body?

> I sat on a gray stone bench
> ringed with the ingenue faces
> of pink and white impatiens
> and placed my grief
> in the mouth of language,
> the only thing that would grieve with me.
>
> —LISEL MUELLER

43

risking dance

And those who were seen dancing
were thought to be insane by
those who could not hear the music.

—Friedrich Wilhelm Nietzsche

When I was a little girl I donned
my invisible gown to dance, spin, and leap like a nymph at the edge
of a secret garden. I don't know when freely moving my body in
dance became fear-laden to me, although it was probably during
junior high, when I was supposed to be "asked to dance." I stood
with the other girls in an awkward line at school parties in the
cafeteria and hoped the right boy would ask me, although I wasn't
sure who that was. I had to be cool, on beat, in the right skirt and
body. For a while I could jitterbug with my popular curly-haired
on-the-beat friend Gail, who was a strong, sure leader, unlike most
of the boys except a few like popular Bruce, king of the hop.

But before long I lost my natural flow. It didn't help that I ended up in a "panty girdle," along with most of us girls in our teens at that amazingly still-Victorian time. I probably weighed all of ninety-eight pounds. Mom told me it wasn't ladylike to "jiggle."

A few years later, a friend invited me to a ballet. It was one of Rudolf Nureyev's first performances in the United States after defecting from Russia's Kirov Ballet. He was paired with the great Dame Margot Fonteyn. Watching the exotic Nureyev leap like a wild animal who was also profoundly human, I was spellbound. I could barely breathe. Margot Fonteyn was otherworldly. I was watching two souls made visible through the dance. The drama and passion made me swoon.

I wanted my body to feel free that way, body beyond physical body as energy and art. I sat there in my panty girdle wanting to fly out of my seat. Instead, aside from swirls and swoops when I was ice skating, I forgot how to move to music.

I was both terrified and excited a few years ago when my friend Tanha challenged me to join her for twelve African dance classes with Jeanne and Larry, fresh from New York, alive and hot with African rhythms. Tanha felt inhibited, too. When she was about twelve, power-striding along, her mom told her that she walked like a man. After that Tanha says she forgot how to walk, much less feel free and powerful within her body.

African dance contained everything my upbringing told me not to do. I felt hopelessly awkward. Shimmy? Not a chance. Determined to learn, I sat on the edge of my bed practicing until I could shake on top without shaking my bottom. Still, I often felt hopeless during class and left in tears more than once.

By the end of six weeks, although still barely following the moves, I realized I'd come upon something essential to my well-being. My marriage was ending and my feelings of sadness were intense. Full-out dance to drums helped me survive what seemed like a fearful loss. I found a way to connect with and contain my flood of emotions and express them with my body. In some ways I think dance has brought me fully into my body for the first time, enlivening my womanliness, my sexuality, my sense of myself as a creature grounded on earth.

Mabiba Baegne, a visiting dance teacher from Congo, explained in a workshop once that in Western culture a person in crisis or breakdown is removed and hospitalized. In African culture the person is taken to the center of the village to be healed in a circle of drummers and dancers.

Now I understand why, in most cultures, dance, song, music, and rhythm are essential parts of coming of age. In dance I think we connect with our own and each other's souls. Dance allows the expression of delight, exuberance, rage, grief. Whatever emotion we're feeling can be moved through the body. Who I am in the world, my full expression, seems connected to my body moving in this way. Although I wasn't aware of this at the time, I think I decided to adopt the dance ritual of another culture to finally allow myself, with children grown and gone, to come of age.

The dances I know—from Africa, the Caribbean, Brazil—involve more than performance and expand my idea of art. The dance and drums are a form of both storytelling and prayer. In Japan, I've read, people don't pray, they dance. When I saw Nureyev leaping free, his dance, both contained and passionate, seemed like prayer to me, a form of communion.

Dance and music can take us to other realms. We listen fully with all our senses. I dance myself right out of my mind. I stay focused in the present moment and allow a larger force to flow through. The impulse to create poetry and art rises from deep within our bodies, I think. Impulse. From the heart, pulse, heartbeat. In dancing we can nourish what's necessary to create and practice other forms of art.

Since those first classes, I crave the sound of drums. I drape myself in sarongs and belts and move from the "center," as Jeanne calls the solar plexus. "We're making the music visible," Jeanne says. "Our feet are drums." The feet connecting in beat with the heart. For a long time I was confused about the arms, watching Jeanne flash across the floor like a bird while I flapped like a broken propeller.

Since returning to dance I've found myself donning my invisible gown again the way I did as a little girl, that is, my invisible sarong and bells. Risking dance, I think now, for me, is about risking life, risking vulnerability, claiming and owning and fully inhabiting my body and power. My larger life inside.

I've learned to dance low and springy, with knees bent. Today Alaine Zinzou from Senegal, regal and warrior-like in dance, showed us how to spring from bent knees in a leap, arms swinging up to help us fly. I found myself springing across the floor, leaping. Well, maybe leap-hopping. Not exactly like Nureyev, but as some sort of earthbound, joyful woman-creature, laughing.

WHERE DO YOU NEED to take more risks in your life?

For you, coming alive might not include risking dance, but

we all need physical practices that help us fully inhabit our bodies. If we can begin to move without inhibition, maybe we can feel freer in our writing or painting or music-making—whatever creative practice we choose.

Find a physical activity you like: tennis, swimming, Rollerblading, surfing. And give dance a try. Buy clothes that make you feel like dancing. Collect music with a beat that calls forth dance. Buy a jangly belt, an ankle bracelet. A belt or cloth low over my hips helps me dance from the "center." Sign up for any kind of dance class that appeals to you—belly dance, tap, tango, salsa, samba, hip-hop, swing, ballroom—and stay for a series of lessons if you can. You may be an awkward beginner like I was.

A nonthreatening and enlivening way to begin dancing (alone or in a group) is with Five Rhythms, developed by dancer/healer Gabrielle Roth. According to my Scottish friend Linda Hummel, "Five Rhythms is a meditative movement practice with no predetermined steps or movements. It's about connecting with the heartbeat and allowing a series of rhythms and energy (flowing-staccato-chaos-lyrical-stillness) to move through you in what together is called a Wave. At the core of the practice is physical grounding, learning to follow your feet and find your roots, trusting, letting go, finding an expression for the soul in its many forms by embodying each rhythm."

If you can find a way, experience the Wave. Meanwhile, walk, swing your arms, swim, jog, fence, spin, practice yoga, whatever allows you to use all of your body. And when it wants, let your body—yourself, your soul—laugh and cry and wail out loud.

.

Your body is the ground and metaphor of your life, the
expression of your existence. It is your bible, your
encyclopedia, your life story.
Everything that happens to you is stored and reflected in
your body. In the marriage of
flesh and spirit, divorce is impossible.

—GABRIELLE ROTH

Many people treat their bodies as if they were rented
from Hertz—something they are using
to get around in but nothing they genuinely
care about understanding.

—CHUNGLIANG AL HUANG

44

....

ooti and vov

·

We have no art. We simply do everything
as beautifully as we can.
—BALINESE SAYING

Near a small lake at a village-like
African dance camp in the local foothills, my friend Tanha and I
talked about our dreams of living in a village. We began to define
what we wanted. Homes in a circle, Mediterranean style, with bal-
conies and walkways. Red roofs, I tossed in, olive trees and a view
of water. I wish I'd asked for a creek or sea. I ended up overlooking a neighbor's funky doughboy pool from my balcony over the
village back fence. Olive trees hide it now.

I remembered standing years earlier on the back steps of our
chartreuse house in Turlock, California, when my kids were toddlers, wishing we were part of a community. Going it alone in a
small family didn't seem natural. I think it truly does take a village

to raise a child. Last month, when I asked a friend with a broad view of human history what we can do to help the world now, he said, with his eyes wide and arms in the air, "Build community. Build community. Build community."

In one version of the local Maidu creation myth, World Maker descends from the heavens on a rope of feathers to join Turtle on a raft on an endless ocean with his fool-clown-like friend Peiheipe. World Maker needs a bit of earth to begin, and sends Turtle to collect mud at ocean bottom. After months underwater, Turtle gasps to the surface. All the mud he gathered has been washed away. World Maker scrapes a tiny speck of dirt from under Turtle's claws into his palm, all he needs. He invites Turtle and Peiheipe to dream and call the earth into being. Together they imagine it round, green, with creatures like *talulu,* squirrel, and *kasakasa,* blue jay. As they sing and call, the speck in World Maker's hand swells into a growing sphere until they're heaved onto a beach at ocean's edge. World Maker gives them sacred *ooti,* acorns, seeds of the great oak to sustain themselves and the other creatures.

Not long after dreaming together about creating a village, Tanha and I became part of a small group dedicated to creating a co-housing community. We met for years in a circle using the consensus process. My marriage was ending, my near-grown kids were leaving, but my village was emerging. Soon I found myself making choices for a small house. The roof was going up just as the cover for my book *poemcrazy* was being designed.

Elisabeth and I blessed the ground at all four corners of the house and buried treasures under the foundation. Now I live in a

.

large oval of thirty families, Valley Oaks Village, all facing inner courtyards with native plantings, bringing us together. We're surrounded by oaks and their acorns—*ooti*—in a native-size community created from the ground up—or, perhaps, from the heavens down.

I wonder if we draw to us what we love. When I was a young girl I often walked to the bus after school past a beloved giant oak, my favorite childhood tree. The oak's still there, round and glorious. Now I live in a village of giant oaks and *ooti*. Poppa told me once that in natural forests, trees and especially oaks grow just the right distance apart so that when they're grown their branches intertwine. In storms and strong winds they hold each other up.

Time and again I see this happen within our small village. We help one another with new babies, illnesses, and death. We love and care for each other's children and provide fellowship that helps hold even rocky marriages together. We still gather in circles to work everything out, listening, making sure each person is heard, using the powerful process of consensus.

When spider webs unite they can tie up a lion.

—ETHIOPIAN PROVERB

BEGIN SMALL. It's not always possible to create an entire village. Find part of your home to transform. My first pottery studio was our large sunny bathroom in an upstairs apartment after Kent and I married. Is there somewhere you can make a small studio for yourself? It helps not to be overly fussy.

·

In Turlock the kids and I turned a hallway into a gallery of framed family photos for Kent's birthday once. Find even a corner where you can make a photo display, a gallery, or an altar.

Write a description of your ideal home. Use color, detail, and landscaping.

My friend Luise Kimme moved to Tobago, West Indies, and bought a bit of land years ago. With local workers and expansive ideas she created a studio that's become a white castle with wooden birds perching on eaves outside and larger-than-life-size dancing figures carved from logs, some now cast in bronze. It's become the Kimme sculpture museum.

When I was finishing a degree in art and writing, my friend Jim Karman suggested I be like the water buffalo. To ford a river without getting stuck, the water buffalo needs only to keep the slightest motion forward. If it stops entirely it gets stuck in the bottom mud. I've never forgotten that image. It's helped me write this book.

If you can gather and create a studio or business or village with others, all the better. We can begin to build community over tea with a friend, dreaming one step at a time. Friends dreamed for years of a quirky café and finally created Chico's beloved local Café Flo, with funky comfortable chairs, whimsical mosaic entry-way, artfully lit gallery walls, music, and the playful Gardner family around and about, cooking and ministering to all of us.

On a larger scale, visionaries like William McDonough are designing huge villages. He's working on one being built in China for three million people, sustainable for basic human needs, with grass on the roofs, energy created on the spot, a central place for elders—everything humans need to live on earth in a new way. Visit the yearly Bioneers Conference (www.bioneers.org), a gathering of people like McDonough creating positive solutions to the various pickles we humans are in. Biologist John Todd says what we need is "human ingenuity wedded to the wisdom of the wild."

Visit Burning Man, a fabulous transformational circular village of more than thirty thousand people creating art, bicycling, and reimagining the world near the end of every summer. Burning Man appears for ten days in the Black Rock Desert of Nevada. The heart of it is radical inclusiveness and sharing. The mind- and heart-expanding world disappears in a festival of burning, without leaving a trace. It began on a beach near San Francisco when a few artists gathered to create and play.

Gather in a circle with friends and family. Dream. No holds barred.

> Finally, the best way to fight evil is
> to make energetic progress in the good.
> —*I Ching*

Everything the power of the world does is done in a circle. The sky is round and I have heard that the earth is round like a ball and so are all the stars. The wind, in its greatest power, whirls.
Birds make their nests in circles, for theirs is the same religion as ours. The sun goes forth and goes down again in a circle. The moon does the same and both are

round. Even the seasons form a great circle in their
changing and always come back again to where they
were. The life of a man
is a circle from childhood to childhood.
And so it is in everything where power moves.

—BLACK ELK

45

---

sun dog: flying heart in lost hills

·

The universe is full of magical things patiently
waiting for our wits to grow sharper.
—EDEN PHILLPOTTS

The truth must dazzle gradually
or every man be blind.
—EMILY DICKINSON

I just got a speeding ticket zooming toward Palm Springs down Interstate 5 to a conference on the re-enchantment of the world (based on the ideas of Joseph Campbell on myth). I seriously need re-enchantment, as I overempathize with my daughter, Elisabeth, in New York City who just quit her job. After our talk on the cell phone my speed got out of control.

Okay, I say mindlessly, inside myself, despondent, "bring me a heart in the sky," asking for an enchanted sign from the heavens to help me know this is a loving as well as creative universe, not just a domain heavily patrolled by police. I discourage overuse of hearts and rainbows and angels in writing workshops, but heck, surely a small kinda-heart can be shaped out of the sparse clouds up there. Is it too much to ask?

Just minutes after my request to the heavens for a sky heart, a sun dog shows up—a small halo kind of rainbow caused by the sun reflecting off atmospheric ice crystals (so I've read). Rare, shimmering, literally out of the blue, there's a full sun rainbow daubed on the bottom of a cloud right in front of me like a multi-colored carrot to guide me south. Hmm, I think, maybe the Great Spirit finds hearts and rainbows interchangeable, the way little girls do in their drawings.

Well, this is amazing. I've been given a sun-dog mini-rainbow when there's no rain. Soon I notice the sun-dog cloud is kind of a flying heart shape, like angel wings in clouds suggesting feathers. I call Bopper back on my cell phone and, watching my speed this time, describe the sky.

Bopper's walking in Manhattan, staring down, she tells me, and hey, she sees a rainbow, too! It's in an oil slick. That's about all New York City can offer at this point, we decide, with no sky to speak of above buildings on a heavy June day.

Well, I say cheerily, it counts as a rainbow. The universe is smacking us upside the head with messages, I add, and we don't see them. Just then, believe it or not, a pigeon swoops low and slaps Elisabeth's head with the tip of its wing. It got her on the nose, she yells into the phone. A wing! This is too much. Urban miracles. If it's in New York, it's gonna be a pigeon and an oil slick, we laugh and stave off hysterical giggles. We talk about my messages from birds, especially blue jays tapping on the walls of my house when I wake up panicky.

Now, outside my window, the sun-dog heart-face floats in clouds like two pony creatures in the sky. It seems the world's showing me that it truly *is* enchanted, alive and creative, whether I see it or not. Wake up, please, sleeping Sue.

The world speaks to me through images, I'm reminded again and again, especially if I initiate the conversation. I must remember to ask. Maybe as we think and imagine, the universe comes creating right along with us. The shrinking sun dog is now the shape of a playful flying bird, its wings a blur of fluttering, or a dolphin, or a manta ray fading to pink gold. Good-bye, darling, I say into the sky, a little teary as I curve down the exit. Thanks for hanging out with me.

> If I wear a green bough in my heart
> the singing bird will come.
> —CHINESE PROVERB

ONE DAY BY THE CREEK my friend Maria and I flooded ourselves with the color of a persimmon and the sun's luminous orange, drenching our eyelids and moving into what seemed to be the living source of color. We spun and intoned what might have been a prayer-chant of the ancient Essenes, E Yah Oh Way, Ee Yah Oh

Way, Ee Yah Oh Way. We offered our own prayer, laughing, spinning, calling out our gratitude.

In our playful ritual mode, invoking nonchalance, calm, dizzy, and with hearts engaged, we heard a startling splash in the shallows behind us, something large and alive. We swung around and there it was, fierce primordial life energy battling upstream: a lone, giant Chinook salmon, living orange, inching along the creek's edge, navigating with an ancient mariner's body memory. We followed, entranced by the unearthly, magical creature we seemed to have conjured in our meditation and playful chanting, immersed in sunlight and in the heart of creation.

Invite a friend to play with sound and color. Create a ritual together. Take turns leading each other in expressing feelings and dreams through sound and movement. Create body prayers and imagine yourself, with great thanks, in the state of being the prayer fulfilled. Do this in a spirit, as Maria and I call it, of "amazing frivolity."

> We have sought for firm ground and found none.
> The deeper we penetrate, the more restless
> becomes the universe; all rushing about and
> vibrating in a wild dance.
> —MAX BORN

46

high hopes:
the mermaid's daughter

•

"I want to buy you a mink," Mom tells me. "Would you like a mink coat?" We're giddy just two days after her risky brain shunt surgery. She has two holes in her head and a hole in her abdomen, and at the age of eighty-seven, she's getting younger before my eyes.

I'm writing at Mom's desk on the thirteenth floor with an expansive view of Lake Michigan and south Chicago. We can see starlike shore lights in Indiana. Earlier we watched a low sun catch fire in the windows of a high-rise. Now the moon's up over the museum, sliced in half—a wing, a peach cradle glowing.

I'm writing everything down again, scribbling, salvation for me, bundling experiences into words for this chapter. High Hopes. For the second time Mom asks, "Would you like a mink? I'd love to get you a mink coat! I'm trying to think of something to get you that's wildly extravagant because I'm so grateful." When Mom realized she could walk across the room almost like a normal person last night, she was so excited she couldn't sleep. We were both ecstatic. "I never really wanted a mink coat myself," Mom says. "I wish I could say it's because I don't believe in killing animals, like you," she muses, "but it's because I look so fat in them." Mom knows I don't want a mink, but she teases, "Would you like a beaver? A raccoon? A Persian lamb?"

I catch her words in my laptop, noticing all my practices coming together in these intense weeks with Mom before and after her surgery. I've been jog-singing and gathering for collage along the sand on the beach. I've been twisting in yoga near the couch after spinning and sprawling in The Five Tibetans—a new/ ancient fountain-of-youth fad. I do my twenty-one spins, leg and head lifts, camel pose, table top, face up dog to cobra. I've been meditating, praying—especially with my Elisabeth—dancing, playing in my ongoing life-sustaining journal, and even making a gigantic concoction of Underground Soup for Mom and me.

Throughout all our time together, even in the rain, I slip outside to walk, swim, gather, write. Looking back it seems I've rushed all my practices into a steady flow to stay balanced during our stressful time. Now that Mom's thriving, my work doesn't seem all that serious. It probably never has been. I can make things sound serious and arty, but truly what I've been doing—not only all this time but all my life, I must confess—is playing.

I'm just beginning to realize how much I like—indeed, need—to play.

Mom and I have done lots of silly singing together. Two days before surgery, lolling with her in bed—the one place she felt okay—Mom said, "How does that song go? The one about high hopes?" The words came to us from the old movie we saw when I was a kid, and we sang together, waving our arms with gusto, about that little old ant who tried to move a rubber tree plant, "Anyone knows an ant, can't, move a rubber tree plant."

Then we came up with our own version of the chorus, "He had high hopes, he had high hopes, he had high, apple pie in the sky, hopes." Mom and I were delighted that the ant managed to do the impossible and move a rubber tree plant.

I'm not always as nice as I'd like to be. In frustration and sadness I called Mom a walrus several years ago when she first lay beached and nearly helpless on the bed. To satisfy my need to be a kind person, I quickly shifted from walrus to the more attractive term mermaid. Mom began to call herself the mermaid. She became the mermaid to our whole family, and small glittery mermaid gifts now bask on her desk and on windowsills and shelves of her apartment. Mermaids might be beautiful, but they don't do well on land. Being a mermaid somehow made Mom's declining condition just a bit less dire, a bit more humorous. And humor, sister to play, might well be one of the most important forms of creativity.

Just before Mom's surgery we planned a getaway.

"Where can we go?" I asked.

"To Ishpeming," Mom said, without hesitation.

"I don't know where Ishpeming is," Mom added. "But that's where we'll go."

I remember Poppa's e-mails to me labeled in Yiddish, *"Ish*

kabibbly schmegegge." Words like *Ishpeming* run in the family, although most of the others are Yiddish: *schlump, spiel, schmooze.* *Verschlugener* is a favorite. Yiddish may well have been devised for coping and lightening things up, for helping us through whatever it is we must get through. Playfully. *Shlemiel, schlemazel, schmaltz,* even *schmuck.* How can you be serious in the face of such wildly creative and ridiculous words? Who first called a belly button a *pippicle?*

More and more over the years, Mom and I play together. Yes. Playing is my favorite creative practice. To heck with poems, boxes, books, the "product." Mom and I are like two stowaway kids near the top floor of her retirement community. When she came home with sloppy "schmaty" bandages flapping from her head two days ago, I sang to her in Yiddish, lying down head to head, *"O mein keppele tut mir weh, O mein keppele tut mir weh,"* Oh my head hurts, oh my head hurts, even though, amazingly, Mom's head with two holes and a drain in her brain didn't hurt much. She was too happy for her head to hurt. And she let me know she doesn't like Yiddish.

Both movies and songs helped us. Almost daily before the surgery Mom broke my heart referring to Humphrey Bogart's words in *Casablanca* to Ingrid Bergman: "We'll always have Paris." We saw the classic movie with Dan last month.

"We'll always have Paris," Mom said one more time the night before her surgery, referring to our close, good time together.

After deciding on her own to risk this surgery, an operation her doctors wouldn't recommend, she said bravely, "Whatever happens, dear, you know I've had a wonderful life."

Famous in our family for her indecisiveness, Mom never waffled on this life-and-death decision. Helping organize her papers, I found a yellow note with her scribbled words: *dementia,* spelled *dimentia,* barely legible, trailing off. This was her fear as her condition worsened rapidly. Mom's always been a spelling-bee queen.

When my hospital-smart sister-in-law, Mary, arrived to be there for the surgery, with John and Rich on call as needed, I noticed that Mom could barely hold a fork, write, walk, get up, sit down. She was *verklemmt. Vermischt.* More Yiddish words that mean what they sound like.

The night after surgery, before we went to sleep, I was worried when she asked, confused, "Will I see Julian in the morning?" I can't remember how I replied.

Nevertheless, I found myself African dancing like a fool next to the soups and sweet rolls in the Au Bon Pain upscale hospital café to help release tension. Thank God for dance to help express my manic state after Mom survived.

The next day everything went wrong. Mom thought she'd had a stroke, couldn't lift her arm. She ate killer hospital pork sausages and pancakes even though the doctor ordered liquids that never appeared. Not the ideal first meal after two days with no food and a tube draining mystery brain stuff into her stomach. I wanted her to sip nectar from the center of a flower. I lost it that morning. Feeling upset and furious, I flew out of the hospital. Yes, *solvitur ambulando.* It is solved by walking.

Like a huge bee drawn to a bed of pansies, I squatted on a

stoop and pulled out my journal. My forever thank-God-for-you little black book. I started to breathe. I pinched petals from nearby pansies and taped them to float about the page like confused wings, purple and yellow, a little torn. Askew. Like me, irate to near hysteria about the food Mom ate without listening to me, furious at her for needing me, for not being better. I taped one pansy in a pinwheel clump, edges slightly folded, perplexed, the way I felt. Heading back to the hospital, I stole twenty-one pinkish petals from cone flowers and taped them like tidy notes in a musical score. This symmetry of petals calmed me enough to return to the hospital room and focus on what to do now. Images in my journal provide a kind of shorthand, I see. There are very few words from these past days. Regardless of my mood, thanks to my journal, I was still playing.

Wise Doctor Penn sent us home. Soon Mom's head began to clear and miracles began to happen. I sensed Mom, who had been increasingly disembodied since Poppa died, shifting back into her body. We were all lightening up. A friend arrived, near tears with joy, among a series of weepy friends. That evening, the day after surgery, Mom already looked great to me, even with two goofy *pachekadic* white gauze bandages flapping over the glued-shut holes in her head. She had a lump like Ray Bolger (as the Scarecrow) after the Wizard of Oz gave him a brain. Tears were starting to flow. Even my brother Rich cried when he saw Mom in the next shift after I left, he told his wife.

That night I listened to the Bee Gees singing "How can you mend this broken heart of mine" sent in an e-mail from a friend accompanied by a slide show of glorious surreal paintings. Somehow art can trigger release. The song and images started me sobbing. I rushed into bed with Mom and lay in awe of the miracle that she was coming back to herself.

Maybe our greatest creative act, our creative challenge, is to find a way to open ourselves to continual renewal.

I'm back running at the lake, spinning like a fool, with expansive thoughts. Tiny shells crunch under my bare feet in the wet sand. I gather wings from monarch butterflies washed onto shore. They've been migrating through Chicago and even in death they're tough enough to hold together in stormy waves amid a flutter of gull feathers. Taped in my journal, these celebration monarch wings express jubilation. And in tonight's dusk I see Mom high up in the window in her paradise peach shirt. She's younger now. I'm spinning crazily, and Mom's waving.

> Though I lack the art
> to decipher it,
> no doubt the next chapter
> in my book of transformations
> is already written.
> I am not done with my changes.
> —STANLEY KUNITZ

47

···

world as studio

·

HITCHHIKER

With its ocean, velvet
drapes, leafy feathers,
father obsession,
its Hebrew chants, Baruch
and Ribbono Shel Olam,
with its Aramaic, abracadabra
Hungarian Bulgarian Yiddish
Litvak Polish
with its Sappho's evening
bringing all things
the bright dawn has scattered,
with its rain, dusk whirlwinds funneling
its grapevine slammed with snow,
with its Bopper, Daniel, Ethel
Julian, John and Richard,

with its cougars, quince, parrots,
mud, cobblestones
knocking on the bottom of its river,
with its primeval jungle gates,
its wind voice, its dimestore dream
marching out with boots,
books of poems, magic
tape, skinny lines of black
ink encircling four
leaf clovers, tumbling,
emitting rays
in a spiraling free-
for-all hum,
my heart
is hitchhiking
home.

—S.W.

48

the only gold

·

All things come from nowhere! How vast,
how invisible, no way to explain it!
—CHUANG TZU

The path to Wisdom Beach is muddy today and blocked by a downed alder. Emma and I scramble past on trampled blackberries. Acorns are everywhere and I want to fill a box with their caps. The acorns, like foolsgold, remind me of all that's hidden in plain sight. Each damp acorn, splitting at the tip, carries a giant oak ready to root and grow.

I make two rows of the cap cups in a long box that held worry beads from Greece. And, as always at Wisdom Beach, the spot with the best mini-litter, I find everything I need. Now one acorn cap holds a curled strip of gold foil and another a crumble of chartreuse from a Nerf football. Since the box came with worry beads I notice I'm unusually free of worry. The acorn cups hold promise, possibility, delight, the depths of nature and I'm with them, especially the empty ones. Free. Nothing's right or wrong. I'm just here, for now, a round open cup gathering surprises, letting wind and rain come my way, letting the day move around me. I realize all's well—a state of being the creek helps me enter here, now, sitting in the roots of a sycamore, where, in morning light, everything's becoming gold.

Emma and I leave only one acorn cup empty, like a blank rune, an open fortune, full of possibility, and now the others seem notably full. Maybe this acorn cup, like me, is waiting to see what the world will drift down to land near the creek first thing tomorrow.

Until then, I write in my journal, *radiant blessings to you.*

With love,

Susan

Love is the only gold.

—ALFRED, LORD TENNYSON

A B O U T   T H E   A U T H O R

•

Susan Wooldridge is the author of *poemcrazy: freeing your life with words* (Three Rivers Press, Random House) and a chapbook of poems, *Bathing with Ants* (Bear Star Press). She leads writing and creativity workshops independently and through the Poets & Writers organization. Susan lives in a co-housing village in Chico, California.

Visit her website, www.susanwooldridge.com.

shok

Godjil

...uring my
Creating process
with you in the hope
that it may spark yours....

...k - in W-3 practice

Move up Burning Man
and Wolf and Wanda
Clock's Breath